The Time of Your Life

The Time of Your Life

LAWRENCE and DIANA OSBORN

Foreword by Peter Brierley

DARTON·LONGMAN+TODD

First published in 1993 by
Darton, Longman and Todd Ltd
1 Spencer Court
140–142 Wandsworth High Street
London SW18 4JJ

© 1993 Lawrence and Diana Osborn

ISBN 0–232–52015–1

A catalogue record for this book is available
from the British Library

Scripture quotations
are from The Holy Bible, New International Version,
copyrighted 1973, 1978, 1984
International Bible Society, published by Hodder & Stoughton

Cover design by Leigh Hurlock

Phototypeset by Intype, London
Printed and bound in Great Britain
at the University Press, Cambridge

Contents

Foreword by Peter Brierley	vii
1 Time Under Pressure	1
2 Biblical and Theological Perspectives on Time	18
3 How Do We Use Our Time?	36
4 Time for Yourself	52
5 Time for Family and Friends	70
6 Time for the World	85
7 Time for Work	100
8 Time for the Church	117
9 Time for God	130
Notes	145

Foreword

I sometimes ask church leaders, 'What resources do you have?' and the answers are given (and expected!) in terms of church buildings or facilities, numbers of members, the available finance, strength of leadership teams, or details of programmes. This book bypasses such conventional answers and substitutes the most important: the hours in our day.

Time management is frequently taught in the context of setting goals, working out priorities, and formulating plans. These are important and valid, and the authors do not despise such methods. But Lawrence and Diana Osborn see such use of time in the context of all the time we will ever have all 24 hours of each day, all 365 days of each year, and all the years of our life.

Lying behind such a concept of time are two complementary elements: our need to know God better, and our need to know God's purpose (or vision) for our lives. The well-known text 'Where there is no vision the people perish' is both true as it stands and as it might be rephrased 'Where there is no vision you and I perish'. Knowing what the Lord would have us do with our lives is a crucially important question, which many find difficult to answer, especially those under thirty years of age.

One part of our difficulty is our segregation of our Christian life (reflected in going to church and attending church meetings) and our working life (seen as the hours for which we are paid a salary). A 1993 survey of lay people heavily involved with their church showed an alarming distancing of these two aspects of our lives. We have to come to appreciate that God is in all

FOREWORD

our lives. This book helps us find the minutes to enjoy his creation and the friends he gave us, to take the opportunities for using our gifts and skills, to relax with our family or neighbour, to meet a stranger, and to pray more for the world in which we live.

The same study showed also the commitment of lay people in the service of their church. Pope John Paul II once said, 'Let not the work of the Lord get in the way of the Lord of the work.' This book is a manual to help us do just that.

It also stresses not only the quantity of time spent but the quality of time invested. The phrase 'do not fill time but fulfil time' is a message that many busy Christian leaders, ordained or lay, and many over-occupied church members should take to heart. Lawrence and Diana Osborn show us how!

PETER BRIERLEY

1

Time Under Pressure

Alice sighed wearily. 'I think you might do something better with the time,' she said, 'than wasting it asking riddles with no answers.'

'If you knew time as well as I do,' said the Hatter, 'you wouldn't talk about wasting *it*. It's *him*.'

'I don't know what you mean,' said Alice.

'Of course you don't!' the Hatter said, tossing his head contemptuously. 'I daresay you never spoke to Time!'

'Perhaps not,' Alice cautiously replied: 'but I know I have to beat time when I learn music.'

'Ah! That accounts for it,' said the Hatter. 'He won't stand beating. Now, if you only kept on good terms with him, he'd do almost anything you liked with the clock. For instance, suppose it were nine o'clock in the morning, just time to begin lessons: you'd only have to whisper a hint to Time, and round goes the clock in a twinkling! Half-past one, time for dinner!'[1]

Our experience of the passage of time is highly subjective. It is proverbial that the rate at which it passes changes with age: time apparently passes more slowly for children. The passage of time is also affected by our hopes and fears. The seconds seem to tick away more rapidly when we anticipate something unpleasant. They slow to a crawl when something pleasant approaches. At times we may even cease to be aware of time's passage altogether.

But whatever our experience of time, it is an inescapable

feature of human life. It characterizes every aspect of our lives: our work, our leisure and our relationships all unfold within time.

Time is the medium in which we live our lives. Thus it is also the medium in which we encounter God and relate to him. The great Reformer, John Calvin used to speak of creation as the theatre of God's glory. Time is such a fundamental part of creation that we might say time is the theatre of God's glory: time is the stage upon which God's glory is revealed and our relationships with God and each other are played out.

THE WESTERN ATTITUDE TO TIME

Because time is so fundamental, the attitude we adopt to it will have far-reaching effects. It will leave its mark upon everything we are and do. According to the theologian Robert Banks, 'If our attitude [to time] is flawed, then all that we are and hope to become, along with everyone and everything we touch, will be flawed also.'[2]

An important factor in shaping that attitude will be the culture in which we live: for most of our readers it will be the technological culture of modern western society. Many influences have gone into shaping the dominant attitude to time in our culture. Because of technological advances we are able to keep track of time in fractions of seconds rather than in hours. The impact of utilitarian ethics on our culture has created the belief that time is a commodity: 'time is money.'

One theme which occurs repeatedly in the literature of our culture is the association of time with death, decay and imperfection. That theme is part of our classical heritage, e.g., the Roman poet Ovid described time as 'the devourer of everything.'

Shakespeare clearly had similar views of time. Like Ovid he speaks of time as 'devouring'. He describes it as an abyss into which we fall or a shoal upon which we are shipwrecked. Time is envious; time is a liar; time is a whirligig; time is a murderer; time is a slut; and time is a thief. A glance at any dictionary of quotations will reveal that similar sentiments about time can be found throughout English literature.

This negative view of time has even found its way into Christian worship. One of the best known English hymns includes the verse

> Swift to its close ebbs out life's little day;
> Earth's joys grow dim, its glories pass away;
> Change and decay in all around I see:
> O thou who changest not, abide with me.[3]

Time is the medium of life but our cultural heritage seems to place a great deal of emphasis on the fact that it is finite. Time runs out. Time may be our life but its passage spells our death. With such images of time firmly entrenched in our cultural heritage it is small wonder that we feel ambivalent about it.

TIME UNDER PRESSURE

Because our time is finite, many of us live with a permanent sense that we do not have enough time. One of the standing jokes in our family for the past several years has been that we would write a book on the problem of time when we could find the time.

Not only does there seem to be little time but what little we have seems to be increasingly regulated by the clock. We once met an Anglican curate who took this regulation of his time to the extreme of timing his hospital visits! Imagine the feelings of those he visited when an alarm went off after fifteen minutes and he moved on to the next case!

a. Increased choice

One factor which puts pressure on our time is the increasing complexity of the modern western lifestyle. This is symbolized by the dramatic increase in consumer choice which has taken place during our lifetime.

In part, this is due to the dramatic technological advances of the past forty years. We are currently trying to choose a new computer. The one on which this chapter is being written is nearly ten years old and was the only one we could afford with the power to do what we wanted it to do. Today we are faced with literally hundreds of options, all slightly different, with different strengths and weaknesses. The choice of software is also bewildering. Instead of the simple decision of a decade ago, we are faced with a complex and time-consuming problem.

Of course not all of the increase in consumer choice is due to technological advance. Take a look round any supermarket. Where we shop, the fish counter now offers breaded hoki while the fruit department stocks a wide range of tropical products which were unknown to us a decade ago. There has been a similar explosion in the variety of toys available for our children. Today when they ask 'What can I play with now?' they probably do not mean 'I've played with all my toys. I'm bored!' Instead they may mean, 'Shall I play with Sindy, or the Sylvanians, or My Little Pony, or the Nintendo, or . . .?'

Such increases in consumer choice imply corresponding increases in the time required to make responsible decisions. Things have certainly come a long way since Henry Ford commented of his cars, 'You can choose any colour, as long as it is black.'

b. Increased rate of change

Our personal problem with choosing a computer touches on another dimension of the time pressure problem. Computers have transformed the way in which information is handled by our culture. The rate of transfer of information is becoming more rapid with every week that passes.

Whereas increased consumer choice affects our private and public lives more or less equally, the increasing rate of information transfer is most obvious in the world of work and, particularly, in the white-collar section of the work force. It is the clerks, the managers and the bureaucrats who are most directly affected by this change. However, the impact on them has an indirect effect on the rest of the work force.

A good example of the change was the computerization of the London stock exchange. The immediate result of that change was a massive increase in the volume of dealing. Far from reducing the workload, the new technology greatly increased its amount and complexity.

c. Over-full lives

The effect of this ever-increasing complexity in every area of our lives is to fill our days with more and more activity. Indeed many people in the first world are in danger of overfilling their lives!

This is most obvious in the workplace. It used to be said that we were moving towards an era of leisure, that machines and computers would take over much of what humans once did. The reality now appears to be very different from that science fiction vision. On the contrary, middle and upper echelon workers are expected to display a degree of commitment to their work which entails long hours. To be successful people must be prepared to achieve results – and the level of expectation always seems to rise. If that means managers have to work late every evening and take work home with them at the weekends so be it. Today, those who are fortunate enough to have work may well find that they have too much of it. The toll in terms of fatigue, workaholism and burn-out is only too familiar.

A corollary of this excess of work is that we have too little time for genuine leisure. Quite apart from the encroachment of work itself into our leisure hours, those who overwork attain such levels of stress that they need more and more time to unwind before they can begin to enjoy their leisure.

Little wonder that many of us succumb to the temptation to do two or three things at once. One Christian writer confesses that

> Before going to work in the morning I would be eating my breakfast at the same time as I was reading the newspaper while also trying to listen to news and commentary from the radio! There was no Sabbath in that life, none of the peace that comes from putting a stop to the endless hurry to catch up.[4]

How many of us are trying to play 'catch-up' in our work and our leisure? How many of us attempt to read and listen to the radio at the same time? How many of us have succumbed to that temptation of television addicts, to watch with a finger on the remote control in an effort to keep track of two or more programmes simultaneously?

d. The effects of time pressure

Modern pressures on our time mean that we do not have enough time for ourselves or for others (for our family, our friends, society and even God). Clearly this lack of time can only have a detrimental effect on every aspect of our life.

Time pressure has an impact on our physical well-being through a number of channels. There is less time to relax, less time for exercise, less time to eat unhurriedly. Sheer lack of time is compounded by the fact that our lives are increasingly regulated by clocks. Clock time ignores the natural rhythms of the body. The result is that very often we find ourselves fighting against our bodies in order to produce results to some unnatural schedule. Yet another casualty is sleep. The net effect is what

Paul Tournier called a 'universal fatigue' afflicting modern society.

Time pressures also have serious implications for thought and personal decision-making. The increasing complexity of our society means that more time is needed and less time is available for responsible thought and decision-making. The result is that in many areas of our life we abandon responsibility for our choices and even our opinions. Advertizers and sales personnel will gladly make our decisions for us. Media gurus and politicians offer us ready-made slogans instead of taking up our time with rational argument.

As we shall see in subsequent chapters, similar comments could be made about the impact of time pressures on personal relationships, public life and our relationship with God.

THE TIME WORSHIPPERS

Chronic shortage of time leads many to become obsessive about time. Time becomes an object of worship – a vengeful surrogate god who has to be placated at every opportunity. Jonathan Swift's Lilliputians certainly saw this as a possibility: they made the following comments about Gulliver's pocket watch,

> we conjecture it is either some unknown animal, or the god that he worships; but we are more inclined to the latter opinion, because he assures us ... that he seldom did anything without consulting it: he called it his oracle, and said it pointed out the time for every action of his life.[5]

A similar comment could be made about the diary or personal organizer. Consider the impact of its loss on the everyday life of a typical busy middle-class western man or woman. The holy book of the modern world is the Filofax!

The nature of religious worship depends upon the character of the object of worship. Time is an impersonal quasi-divine force which imposes itself on our lives. And the ways in which modern secular men and women seek to deal with the problem of time bear a striking similarity to the strategies devised by our pagan forebears to cope with a cosmos shot through with threatening divine forces. The most popular strategy was the way of magic: our ancestors came to terms with threatening cosmic forces by finding ways of controlling and manipulating them. In relation to time, the magical talisman of our society is the labour-saving device and the magical ritual is the latest time management technique.

a. The myth of the labour-saving device

One common misconception of our technology dominated society is that we can find technological solutions to our time problems; that, if the right technological talismans are available we will be able to control our time more effectively. At one time it was a commonplace of futurological speculation that labour-saving devices would provide us with more free time and transform our society into a leisure society.

In retrospect such predictions seem naively optimistic. The economist E. F. Schumacher even goes so far as to suggest that

> the amount of genuine leisure available in a society is generally in inverse proportion to the amount of labour saving machinery it employs. If you would travel, as I have done, from England to the United States and on to a country like Burma, you would not fail to see the truth of this assertion.[6]

Two factors undermine the labour-saving potential of labour-saving devices. One is the acquisitive nature of the modern western lifestyle. Any time which is saved by genuine labour-saving devices is rapidly eroded by the need to service our acquisitions. The more we possess, the more time is required to maintain our possessions and the less time we have to enjoy our leisure.

The other, more serious, factor is that while labour-saving devices do, indeed, reduce the time required to do certain chores, that time saving is immediately dissipated by the new possibilities or higher standards created by the existence of the device.

Washing machines and modern fabrics certainly reduce the labour involved in washing the family's clothes. But they have not significantly reduced the amount of time spent on washing clothes because our standards of cleanliness have risen. The average modern family probably generates as much dirty washing in one day as its Victorian equivalent would have produced in a week!

The telephone is widely regarded as a labour-saving device. Advertisements for *Yellow Pages* and similar directories advise us to let our fingers do the walking. It is certainly easier and quicker to contact someone by phone than to write a letter. On the other hand, trying to contact someone whose telephone seems always to be engaged can be frustrating and time-consuming. Even more frustrating are the call stacking devices which make you queue to have your call answered. Granted that telephones generally speed up communication, they may tempt us to increase the number of things we try to do. For example, if we take the advertisers' advice and let our fingers do the walking, we may phone a dozen or more shops to find the best price of some item whereas without a phone we might have limited ourselves to visiting one or two shops. The telephone also makes it easier to increase our circle of superficial acquaintances at the expense of our close friendships.

The motor car, like the telephone, cuts down the time required to do certain things. It makes large shopping expeditions much easier – a weekly or monthly visit to the freezer centre replaces daily trips to the corner shop. It also makes the chauffeuring of children to a much greater variety of activities a practical possibility.

Motor cars, telephones and even washing machines are possibility-creating devices rather than labour-saving devices. By reducing the time of certain chores, they open up new possibilities: higher standards of cleanliness, easier communications, greater mobility. Unfortunately, human nature being what it is, the possible rapidly becomes obligatory.

The possibility-creating device par excellence is the computer. Like the telephone and motor car, the computer certainly makes some tasks easier (e.g., maintaining accurate personal accounts). But, once again, it has opened up new horizons. It allows us to do things we could not have contemplated a decade ago. Consider the following comment on the report of the presidential commission which investigated the space shuttle *Challenger* disaster:

> *everything* had 23 versions. It has been noted that computers, which are supposed to increase the speed at which we do things, have not increased the speed at which we write reports: we used to make only three versions – because they're so hard to type – and now we make 23 versions![7]

Labour-saving devices do not address our time problems. On the contrary, by creating new possibilities, they may actually exacerbate our difficulties.

b. The time management industry

Time management is a more realistic approach than that of seeking some external technological fix. It recognizes that the problem is not purely external; that there is also a personal dimension to the problem. Instead of offering some technological panacea it begins with the person who is experiencing the problems.

The starting point for most time management is self-knowledge. Before you can begin to tackle your difficulties with time in any practical way you must discover how you use your time: how you actually use it, not how you think you use it! Thus most time management techniques begin with the exercise of time logging, keeping a more or less detailed record of what you actually do with your time over periods of from a week to a month or more.

Having opened your eyes to what you actually do, time management then offers a variety of strategies for managing your time more effectively. Most of these are no more than codified common sense. However, the very fact that there is such a great demand for training in what should be common sense once again reveals the extent of the problem we have with time.

We have been using time management techniques in educational and church settings for many years and insights from this quarter will appear frequently in the pages of this book. However, valuable as time management is, it is not a complete answer to the time problems of modern society.

To begin with, the very strength of time management is also a limitation. It tends to stress the personal dimension at the expense of the structural dimension of our time problem. That so many people in so many different walks of life experience difficulties with time strongly suggests that it is not merely the problem of individuals. However, time management does not question the structures and assumptions of the society in which the problems arise. At best it can offer first aid to the casualties of our culture's inadequate views of time.

Thus time management tends to reinforce the status quo. Most time management programmes do not question our culture's obsession with the clock and the diary. On the contrary, they reinforce our dependence upon them. From a Christian perspective, any approach which tends to make an idol out of time must be treated with caution.

Another limitation of time management techniques is that they have evolved in the workplace and tend to be work-oriented. Thoughtless application of such techniques to our leisure time may result in our leisure taking on the character of work. For example, Diana enjoys swimming: time management helps by reminding her to timetable a regular session at the baths. But time management also encourages the setting of goals and this may be less helpful in leisure time!

Finally, time management may create the illusion that we are in control of our time. Thus it may subtly deny our creaturehood. As we shall see later, it is not us but God who is Lord of time.

However, in spite of these limitations, time management remains a valuable tool. If you like, it is a necessary remedial step on the road to developing a new and healthier attitude to time.

THE FLIGHT FROM TIME

An alternative to the attempt to control time is to treat it as an enemy to be evaded or destroyed. This was the strategy adopted by the religions of the classical world. The Greeks regarded time with distaste. For them it was no more than the moving image of eternity – a mere shadow play of illusion which in some vague way reflected the realities of the spiritual realm. The legacy of that view is still a significant force in shaping contemporary western attitudes.

Of course, this is not usually obvious. Few people will openly admit to believing that time is an illusion (although Albert Einstein is reputed to have said, 'Time is an illusion, albeit a persistent one'). Rather the advocates of this strategy will claim an interest in the present while focusing their attention on the past, the future, or some timeless elsewhere.

a. The nostalgia trip

One common way in which people seek to evade the problem of time is to deny the claims of the present by taking refuge in some romanticized past. Nostalgia is big business. Period drama is a highly popular form of television entertainment. Politicians extol 'Victorian values'. Even the relatively recent past is carefully preserved in showcases by such organizations as the National Trust and English Heritage.

One reason for this widespread nostalgia is our longing for a less complex way of life, for a time when change occurred at a more manageable pace, relationships were closer and our lives were less completely regulated by the clock. However, we cannot turn the clock back: we cannot 'dis-invent' the computer or the atomic bomb; we cannot recapture the innocence which knew nothing of Auschwitz or Cambodia.

b. *Utopianism*

Instead of looking backwards many people pin their hopes on some future transformation of society. Instead of taking refuge in a romanticized past, they take refuge in a dream of what the future might hold.

At least part of the attraction of the New Age movement is of this kind. It holds out a promise of an imminent transformation in human society which will sweep away all the old injustices and oppressive structures and replace them with more humane structures in some way which is never fully explained.

But utopianism is by no means limited to New Agers. The commercial success of futurological speculation indicates that many besides the hyper-spiritual minority are placing their hopes in the future. Authors such as Alvin Toffler and Herbert Kahn make a living out of feeding such hopes with fresh images of what the future might hold.

However such flights into the future are just as unrealistic as attempts to take refuge in the past. Of course we must have hopes for the future, just as we must have an awareness of our legacy from the past. But unless both past and future are related to the present they are nothing more than beguiling illusions. It is right to look backwards from time to time – our ancestors may have valuable lessons to teach us (but they must be applied in the present). It is right to have hopes – they give direction to the present (but only if we can see some way of relating the present reality to our future hope).

c. Artificial eternities

Another option besides the flight into past or future is the attempt to step outside time altogether. This is the strategy adopted by various kinds of religious mysticism. Certain spiritual disciplines have been found to break down our consciousness of the passage of time, giving an experience which is interpreted as a taste of (timeless) eternity.

Today this strategy is no longer limited to overtly religious groups. The widespread problem of drug abuse bears witness to an attempt on the part of many in our society to evade the problems of the present by emigrating inwards. Raves and acid-house parties are said to produce a similar effect without the need to take drugs. The New Age commentator, Marilyn Ferguson, cites an amazing variety of potential 'psychotechnologies', techniques for achieving this suspension of temporal consciousness. In addition to drugs, dancing and traditional spiritual exercises, she cites sensory deprivation, biofeedback, artistic activities of all kinds (singing, painting, pottery), theatre and psychodrama, hypnosis, psychotherapy, sport and various kinds of body work (such as the martial arts).

One of the techniques Ferguson cites is storytelling. Retreating into myth can be yet another way of evading the present. This is particularly clear in science fiction and fantasy. A television documentary on the work of the award-winning science fiction writer Anne McCaffrey included interviews with fans who admitted that reading her novels enabled them to escape into a better world. A similar phenomenon can be seen amongst the Trekkies who spend much of their leisure time imagining themselves in the alternative future created by the Star Trek TV series.

To be effective the retreat into myth requires a fairly vivid imagination. But once again the computer revolution looks set to transform things. Over the last decade computer games have become increasingly sophisticated. Today there is talk of computer simulations as virtual reality. If they were addictive a decade ago, how much more addictive will they be by the end of the century?

THE VULNERABILITY OF WESTERN CHRISTIANS

Christians are by no means immune to the time pressures which afflict our culture. Far from it! As if the internal pressures of the secular world of work were not enough, many Christians bring to their work a vestigial (and usually misunderstood) Protestant work ethic. Thus they take their work more seriously than the average person. In addition to their sense of obligation to work, Christians take seriously their obligation to the family and the wider community. Christians are often in the forefront of charitable efforts and pressure groups seeking social justice. Churches and other Christian organizations also place heavy demands upon our time.

Christians today are confronted by too many opportunities for service, too many needs demanding to be met. The inevitable result is a growing sense of confusion, frustration and guilt. Depending on our personality this may lead either to a creeping mental paralysis or an ever-increasing frenzy of activity. We either find ourselves incapable of responding or responding unthinkingly to the most immediate and apparently urgent demands.

If Christian lay people are vulnerable to such pressures, clergy and their families are in a much worse situation. Far from only working one day a week, they are much more likely than lay people to be working seven days a week. A Clergy Training Officer notes the following clergy reactions to the idea that curates should aim to work a forty-eight hour week:

> The incumbents could not stomach this idea at all.... [It] would never work in a big parish; it was their duty to knock this ivory-tower idealism out of their curates and replace it

with a good dose of parochial pragmatism. The word 'lazy' was not used, but it was not far from the surface.[8]

It is almost as if the clergy have distilled the guilt and busyness of ordinary Christians to the highest possible degree. Contemporary theology often speaks of the priesthood as representative of the people of God but one wonders whether guilt and busyness are an appropriate part of such representation?

Unfortunately the notion of burning yourself out for God has gained a certain amount of legitimacy amongst Christians. It has almost become the peculiarly evangelical form of martyrdom. Victorian missionary biographies regale us with tales of brave men of God killing themselves with overwork. What goes unrecorded is the toll imposed upon their families. How many wives killed themselves, dutifully trying to keep up with their husbands? How many children faced years of neglect because their father put his vocation before their needs?

In the chapters which follow we shall argue that this is by no means a biblical approach to the time of our lives. We shall also offer a variety of practical strategies for resisting secular time pressures. However, before we begin, it may be helpful to spend a little time using the following exercises to reflect on the extent to which we are affected by time pressures.

6. Exercises

a. Clock addiction

Most of us suffer from some degree of psychological dependence upon the clock. A simple test is to remove your watch and try to get through the next twenty-four hours without looking at a clock. Given the extent to which our society is addicted to clocks, this exercise is best attempted at the weekend!

Many people find the experience very disorienting. Some will suffer withdrawal symptoms such as irritability, anxiety and inability to concentrate. That is why it is one of the standard techniques used by authoritarian religious sects to manipulate potential recruits.

b. Pressure points

Have there been any moments in the past week/month/quarter when you felt you were too busy, short of time, or overloaded with conflicting demands? If your answer is 'no', congratulations. However, you are probably reading this book because there *have* been times when you wondered how you were going to fit everything into the time available.

Take a few minutes to think about some of those occasions. Try to identify more precisely why you felt too busy (the answer 'not enough time' is not permitted). Did the demands come from others or from yourself? Could they have been anticipated? Did some of them subsequently prove to be less urgent/important than they appeared at the time? Do any of them relate to the time pressures identified in this chapter?

At this stage, the point is merely to become more aware of the pressure points in your own time, to recognize that some are within our control and others are due to other people/society.

c. My times are in your hands

Take a few minutes to reflect on these words of David from Psalm 31. Read the psalm and try to build up a mental picture of his circumstances. Do these words have anything to say to you about your particular time pressures?

2

Biblical and Theological Perspectives on Time

Everyone is excited. Jesus has just returned from a preaching trip. The news spreads like wildfire and a crowd gathers. Expectation mounts. The word goes round that Jairus is coming to Jesus: the ruler of the synagogue, the one whose daughter is seriously ill. What a show!

Jesus agrees to go with Jairus and the crowd follows, pushing and jostling for a good view of the proceedings. They swarm around him, pushing passers-by out of their way. 'Make way! The Master is on his way to Jairus' house! There's no time to be lost.'

Jairus is frantic with worry: will they be in time? The crowd is frantic with anticipation. But Jesus proceeds at his own pace.

Suddenly he stops. He looks around. 'Who touched me?' he asks. Peter, caught up with the impatience of the mob, rounds on him: 'Master, the people are crowding and pressing against you!' But Jesus won't be diverted: 'No, Peter. Someone touched me.'

The crowd has come to a halt around this tableau. What is happening? Why is he just standing there? Who does he think he is, to keep an important man like Jairus waiting – and at a time like this?

Seconds creep by like hours as he stands there waiting. At last she steels herself to admit what she has done. She falls at his feet, mortified that he should stop for a nobody, for a woman who is a virtual outcast. The crowd growls its indignation but quietly Jesus overrules them with his 'Daughter, your faith has healed you. Go in peace.'

We know how the story ends. But notice the contrast between Jesus and the crowd, between his attitude to time and ours. Time was of the essence. Most of us would not allow ourselves to be diverted from an urgent task in this way. That contrast is a good starting point for an examination of biblical teaching about time.

A TIME FOR EVERYTHING

There is a time for everything, and a season for every activity under heaven:
 a time to be born and a time to die,
 a time to plant and a time to uproot,
 a time to kill and a time to heal,
 a time to tear down and a time to build,
 a time to weep and a time to laugh,
 a time to mourn and a time to dance,
 a time to scatter stones and a time to gather them,
 a time to embrace and a time to refrain,
 a time to search and a time to give up,
 a time to keep and a time to throw away,
 a time to tear and a time to mend,
 a time to be silent and a time to speak,
 a time to love and a time to hate,
 a time for war and a time for peace. (Eccles. 3:1–8)

According to Ecclesiastes, life has its seasons and there is a right time for everything in life. Time ebbs and flows; opportunities come and go according to its rhythms. This cyclical experience of time is a universal feature of agrarian societies: the farmer works in harmony with the time and seasons, the rhythms of natural life.

We have lost that harmony with natural rhythms and replaced

it by an unnatural clock time. For us times are not determined by the forces of nature but by arbitrary markings on the clock; mere numbers which bear little relation to nature. Our experience of time is of an inexorable onward rush from one thing to the next. Small wonder that this description appeals so strongly to us.

However, that gentle ebb and flow has an oppressiveness all of its own which is not readily apparent to those of us who are caught in the rapids of twentieth-century clock time. For all its gentleness, the cycle of seasons imposes a regime of iron upon rural life. Seed time, the annual rains, harvest time: they may come round more slowly than the recurring markers of modern life but they demand at least as much obedience as their urban counterparts. For the nature-worshipping contemporaries of the ancient Israelites, the seasons determined not only the work cycle in the fields but the pattern of religious festivals and hence the entire cycle of social and cultural life.

But Ecclesiastes' response to this iron regime is radically different from classical escapism or modern attempts to control time. The writer must have been aware of the negative aspects of time but, nevertheless, can say that God 'has made everything beautiful in its time' (Eccles. 3:11). For Ecclesiastes, as for the author of Genesis 1, time is not a limitation but an integral part of God's creation. Thus creation is dynamic rather than static: nothing is permanent but everything has a time and place in God's purpose.

The sense that there are appropriate times for the various activities of life is one that pervades the Bible. There are right times for specific work-related activities (Gen. 29:7; Isa. 28:24f). More generally, there is a time for work and a time for rest (Jesus uses this metaphorically in John 9:4). There was also a time to travel and a time to remain in one place (Num. 9:15–23; Acts 1:4, 8). The Old Testament even records an appropriate time for making oneself alluring (Esth. 5:1)! Robert Banks sums up this view of time as follows:

all aspects of life have their appropriate times. Some of these come only once, others will recur again and again. It is important to recognise when something is having its particular time and to allow the full interval appropriate to it. The character of the event, experience, stage in life or relationship will determine the type and length of time that should be placed at its disposal.[1]

THE RIGHT TIME

The Israelites were by no means unfamiliar with methods of time measurement. New Testament references (e.g., to the third hour or the sixth hour) indicate the same forms of time measurement as those of the rest of the Roman Empire. However the biblical authors were clearly more interested in the quality of specific times than in the quantitative measure of its passage. Thus, except when it is specifically qualified by an ordinal number, the word 'hour' tends to refer to a specific significant moment in time rather than to any system of time measurement. Their emphasis was very much on knowing the right time. But in what sense did the Israelites understand particular times to be right?

Times were right or appropriate or opportune primarily because they were appointed by God. Thus, above and beyond the natural rhythms of the seasons, they discerned the gracious hand of the God who says, 'I will send rain on your land in its season, both autumn and spring rains, so that you may gather in your grain, new wine and oil' (Deut. 11:14; cf Ps. 145:15; Isa. 49:8; Jer. 18:23). It is this assurance that the apparently endless round of seasons is governed by a caring God that enabled Ecclesiastes to celebrate the ebb and flow of time. The fact that the times are appointed by God is what gives meaning to the passage of time for the biblical authors.

The biblical view of time is sometimes described as linear to distinguish it from the cyclical view of time which stresses the cycle of the seasons. However, it is very different from the linear view of time which has prevailed in the West since the emergence of science. For secular western thought time has been an inexorable onward flow: the whirlpool of seasons has been replaced by the ever-rolling stream. This is not the view of time which emerges from the Bible. Time may be linear in the sense that the purposes of God transcend the circularity of natural rhythms and move creation on towards ever-new possibilities. But that onward movement is not inevitable; it is not an ever-rolling stream. On the contrary, God is active in appointing these times. Thus, instead of a meaningless abstract continuity, the Bible stresses that particular moments are God-given.

Without that assurance, the future offers only insecurity. A favourite phrase of time managers is *carpe diem*: seize the day! Make the most of the present. They forget the original context: 'While we're talking, time will have meanly run on: pick today's fruits [*carpe diem*], not relying on the future in the slightest.' We cannot trust the future. Therefore, since the past is dead, we must pick today's fruits: there is nothing else on which we can rely.

By contrast, the biblical belief in God's sovereignty over time allows believers to be patient. The time appointed by God may be long in coming. It may be the reversal of long years of apparent failure and oppression (Isa. 49:8). It may be the fulfilment of years of obscurity and preparation (e.g., the decades of wandering before the Israelites could enter the Promised Land; the long years of exile; the years in which Jesus grew to manhood before his brief public ministry). It is a salutary reminder in this age of instant results that God sometimes looks for fruit that matures very slowly indeed!

TIME AS GOD'S CREATION

a. The creation of time

One of the most striking features of the account of creation in Genesis 1 is its temporal framework. God's act of creation is built around the days of the week and, in the course of that activity, the fundamental markers of time are defined.

By biblical standards, Benjamin Franklin's dictum that 'time is money' sets far too low a value on time. Time is fundamental to human life in a way that is not true of money (in spite of those who would have us believe that 'money makes the world go around'). Whether or not one takes the days of creation literally, it is clear from Genesis 1 that time is an integral part of creation.

Again the contrast with the classical view of time is clear. For the Greeks, the passage of time was symptomatic of the imperfection of the material world. For the biblical writers, the passage of time was natural: it was part of what made God's good creation good. Interestingly this insistence on the positive value of time is more in keeping with modern developments in physics than with the timelessness of classical physics.

b. Time as the environment of human life

The environmental crisis has made many of us much more aware of our dependence upon the space we inhabit. It is no longer merely space, or wilderness, or even real estate but our environment. Arguably, many of the problems which we have come to associate with the phrase 'environmental crisis' have arisen from our culture's treatment of the environment as a commodity to be exploited rather than as space to be lived in. Thus a hillside is no longer appreciated for what it is but is seen in terms of so many sheep per acre, or the value of the timber growing upon it, or of the minerals which may be extracted from it. And when the 'developers' have finished the hillside may have degenerated from wilderness to desert.

If we adopt the biblical insight that time is also part of our human environment, contemporary pressure on time may be seen as an environmental crisis every bit as destructive as its more commonly acknowledged counterpart. True, the effects of this crisis are less obvious than slag heaps or climatic change but their spiritual and psychological impact is dehumanizing, and they have serious spin-offs for our physical well-being.

Time, as much as space, is our natural habitat. It is the medium in which we work out our most fundamental calling, the calling to be images of God as persons-in-relationship, the calling to be fully human. Contemporary working practices (and cultural expectations) destroy that habitat just as effectively as industrial pollution destroys our physical habitat. The imposition of clock time and our culture's obsession with growth (which, in terms of time, means ever-increasing productivity, higher efficiency, more overtime, fewer holidays, ever-increasing dedication to the job) are corrosive of human relationships. If they are left unchecked such pressures lead inevitably to frustration and dehumanization.

c. *The goal of creation*

The Sabbath appears in Genesis 1 as the goal of creation. This suggests an important principle which will be helpful in developing a Christian response to the contemporary cult of busyness. Created life finds its meaning and fulfilment in the repose of the Sabbath, not in the busyness of the six days. Furthermore the Sabbath rest is anticipated on each of the six days when God steps back from his creative activity and contemplates what he has done. Busy Christians would do well to meditate on the implications of this passage. Too often we mistake busyness in Christian service for Christian commitment. In fact, real commitment may demand that we take more time to stand back from our work and get it in context.

TIME AS GOD'S GIFT

At one point the devil Screwtape offers his nephew the following advice:

> You must . . . zealously guard in his mind the curious assumption 'My time is my own'. Let him have the feeling that he starts the day as the lawful possessor of twenty-four hours . . . The assumption which you want him to make is so absurd that, if it is once questioned, even we cannot find a shred of evidence in its defence. The man can neither make, nor retain, one moment of time; it all comes to him by pure gift; he might as well regard the sun and moon as his chattels.[2]

Genesis 1 tells of God giving dominion to humankind. Verses 26 and 28 are very specific: human dominion extends over the entire biosphere. But the creatures of the first three days of creation are excluded: human dominion does not extend to time and space as such. God gives time to individuals and peoples but he does not give human beings lordship over time: we are its subjects; God is its master.

But God also appoints the times and the seasons of our lives. This combination of emphases gives rise to the recurring Old Testament theme that the years of our lives are given to us by God. One important expression of this theme was the institution of the Sabbath. As Jesus pointed out to the irate Pharisees, 'The Sabbath was made for man, not man for the Sabbath' (Mark 2:27). Far from being a legalistic imposition upon our time, the Sabbath was the gift of respite from the toil which characterizes daily life. It cut across the natural rhythms of the seasons and the otherwise irresistible demands of daily life in an agrarian society. It condemned the idolatry of busyness which would encourage us to work continually to the detriment of family and social life.

a. A gift is not...

Because a gift points beyond itself to a relationship, it cannot be treated as a commodity. A wedding ring is more than the value of the gold it contains. There is more to a gift than its market value. Therefore we should neither hoard our time nor dispose of it thoughtlessly for economic advantage. Rejecting a commodity view of time implies that a legitimate Christian approach will involve generosity. Instead of guarding our minutes jealously we should be prepared to give them generously to others. Thus we should be prepared to be flexible for the sake of others: human relationships are more important to God than impersonal plans or programmes. Since time is the habitat of human relationships we should not allow our clocks and our timetables to encroach upon it.

Similarly, because time is a gift we no longer need to look upon it as an enemy. On the contrary, this qualified giving of something over which God retains dominion, has the potential for bringing us closer to the divine giver. Thus time is not to be avoided or evaded but, rather, to be enjoyed as God's good gift.

b. Enjoying time

Someone once commented that 'time enjoyed is time redeemed.' But what does this mean? Time cannot be enjoyed in the way that we might enjoy a piece of music or a beautiful landscape. Rather time is the medium in which such enjoyment takes place.

Jesus warned his disciples not to be anxious about tomorrow. His point was that God will provide. But anxiety over tomorrow also undermines our enjoyment of the present. I cannot enjoy this walk or that Bruckner symphony if my thoughts are continually jumping forward to that interview tomorrow or next week's visit to the dentist.

Similarly we are unlikely to be enjoying time if we are very aware of its passage. We probably enjoy time best when we are least aware of its passage. Thus 'enjoying time' is paradoxical. Conscious attempts to enjoy time are likely to be counterproductive. C. S. Lewis makes a similar point in *Surprised by Joy*:[3] the conscious attempt to seek out joy inevitably leads to its disappearance. By getting on with life we find that joy surprises us at the most unlikely moments. The same is true of time. Instead of worrying about whether our time is genuinely fulfilled, it is better simply to live life now and let the enjoyment of time surprise us: 'Didn't the time pass quickly!'

This is by no means straightforward in contemporary western society. Cultural pressures tend to force us to live on borrowed time. Instead of living in the present, the busy executive is likely to be living with one foot in next week (or next year). On a personal level, we are continually bombarded by advertising encouraging us to prepare for the future with pension schemes and insurance plans of all sorts.

The temptation to live in the past or the future rather than the present has always been with us. That is why most spiritual traditions have centring exercises as their most basic discipline. Such exercises help us to let go of the past or the future and concentrate instead upon the present. Arguably we are in greater need of such disciplines today than ever before.

One thing is certain, attempts to control our time by means of clocks, engagement diaries and project planners make it more difficult to enjoy that time. There is more to living in time than anxiously controlling it as if it were a potentially dangerous beast of uncertain temper.

c. Respecting time

Another implication of these biblical and theological insights is that time should be respected. It is not ours to control but rather something which God graciously shares with us. Thus time has its own integrity and structures which we should respect rather than ignore.

The times and seasons of our lives have their own natural

rhythms. Contrast the gentle ebb and flow of Ecclesiastes' poem on time with the structureless linearity of the modern attitude to time: a straight line divided into arbitrary segments for the convenience of time-keeping. The dominance of clock-time and the cult of efficiency have to a large extent suppressed time's natural rhythms. The landmarks of our temporal habitat have been bulldozed to make way for artificial substitutes: clocking-on, project deadlines, flight schedules.

But the Bible does not simply adopt a natural cyclical view of time. It introduces a number of other features which we would do well to respect.

(i) Past and future
There is the radical difference in our experience of past, present and future.

Many people view the past as complete; it has passed; it is unchangeable. However, from a biblical perspective, we are not entirely bound by the past: the possibility of repentance and subsequent transformation implies a degree of freedom with respect to personal, family and cultural histories.

In sharp contrast to the past, the future appears open and unstructured: it is the realm of possibilities which may or may not come to pass. But other cultures have supposed the future to be just as determined as the past; just more of the same old thing. There is a hint of this in Ecclesiastes' refrain 'there is nothing new under the sun.' However the dominant point of view which has emerged from biblical and subsequent Christian traditions is that there resides within the future the possibility of radical newness: the new heavens and new earth of the *eschaton* (the last days). It may be new and radical but it is not completely divorced from what has gone before. The future is not entirely free; there are chains of cause and effect which link yesterday to tomorrow. A Christian understanding of time provides a basis for hope in the future.

(ii) Unexpectedness

The openness of the future leads to another aspect of our experience of time which modern pressures may suppress – its unexpectedness. This is often contradicted by the time management approach to life. If God is active in time, then our times are not entirely under our control. God may call us to an activity which continues for years with no apparent results. Consider the pioneer missionary, Fraser of Lisuland: he spent years preaching the gospel to the tribespeople of Lisuland with no apparent results; shortly before he was due to return home, an apparent failure, the people with whom he had been working began to convert to Christianity in large numbers. God's creative activity combines both slowness and suddenness – the dramatic conversion of thousands at Pentecost or in the Welsh Revival and the long, slow, invisible, apparently fruitless faithfulness of men and women through the ages.

(iii) Flexibility

Similarly, although natural rhythms are to be respected as part of God's good creation they are not an iron law. Sometimes God cuts across those regularities. The Sabbath was the most important regular feature of the Jewish timescape but Jesus was prepared to ignore it in order to heal the sick. Indeed his entire ministry was marked by a degree of flexibility which would be regarded as unacceptable in many spheres of modern society.

For example, consider Jesus' final journey to Jerusalem. The climax of his ministry is approaching and he is travelling to Jerusalem by way of Jericho. But he allows himself to be stopped by a blind beggar (Luke 18:35–43). Immediately after that he again allows his progress to be interrupted – this time by a notorious collaborator with the Romans. These people were not 'strategic contacts' whose conversion would aid Jesus' mission in any way. On the contrary, they were the dregs of Jewish society. But Jesus' personal programme was flexible enough for him to find time for them simply because they were needy human beings.

REDEEMING THE TIME

a. Time and sin

Like every other aspect of life, our experience of time is tainted with sin. Instead of accepting it as a good gift of God we are inclined to view the passage of time with dread. One of the most poignant biblical illustrations of the effect of sin on our attitude to time is the story of Martha and Mary:

> As Jesus and his disciples were on their way, he came to a village where a woman named Martha opened her home to him. She had a sister called Mary, who sat at the Lord's feet listening to what he said. But Martha was distracted by all the preparations that had to be made. She came to him and asked, 'Lord, don't you care that my sister has left me to do the work by myself? Tell her to help me!'
>
> 'Martha, Martha,' the Lord answered, 'you are worried and upset about many things, but only one thing is needed. Mary has chosen what is better, and it will not be taken away from her.' (Luke 10: 38–42)

Too many Christians today seem to take Martha as their role model. Perhaps it is because of the popularity of military metaphors for the church: we are seen as conscripts in the army of God, as soldiers on duty, and anything which takes us away from the busyness of ministry is seen as dereliction of duty. Whether or not this is the cause, we have become a church of Marthas constantly fussing over the busyness of life.

Busyness may be a way of evading the claims of others or of God upon our lives. Alternatively, busyness may be an exercise in self-justification. Too often, those of us who claim to be justified by faith are tempted to prove the reality of our justification by being busy for God.

Of course personal sinfulness is only one part of the contemporary time crisis. The structures of our society also play their part. If my boss presses me to work more overtime at the expense of my family, I may be faced with the choice of compliance (and possible promotion or, at least, a degree of security) or possible loss of job during the next round of cuts. Nor is the boss necessarily to blame – he or she is often just another cog in the system as a whole.

b. *The example of Jesus*

As Christians our fundamental model for everyday life is the life and behaviour of Jesus himself. While there are no explicit statements about use of time in the Gospels, Jesus does set us a very clear example throughout his ministry.

The story at the beginning of the chapter shows Jesus resisting the sense of urgency which must have possessed the crowd of onlookers. His encounters with the blind beggar and Zacchaeus show that human need took priority over missionary strategy.

Another example is John's account of the beginning of his ministry. Instead of working hard to make an impact, what does Jesus do? He goes off to a friend's wedding! Jewish weddings were major social events lasting several days. But consider what it means in terms of Jesus' attitude to time. Clearly he felt it was important to take a week's holiday from preaching and casting out demons and all the other things expected of a Messiah in order to have fun with his friends.

There are times, particularly in Mark's Gospel, where you get the impression that Jesus is close to being inundated by the demands and needs of those around him. And yet he never seems to be busy. He always has time for the needy person who comes to him whether that person is a leper, a prostitute, a priest, or an officer of the occupying power. Above all he always has time to take off on his own into the wilderness; he always has time to pray.

c. The call to redeem the time

'Be very careful, then, how you live – not as unwise but as wise, making the most of every opportunity' (Eph. 5: 15f).

Older translations enjoin us to make 'the most of the time' (RSV) or 'redeem the time' (AV, RV). The modern emphasis on busyness may tempt us to read this as an injunction to be always busy (in the Lord's service). But is this what Paul intended? Did he want us to fill every second or fulfil every second?

In the light of what we have already seen of the biblical attitude to time, redeeming the time has more to do with the quality of our experience of time than with its efficient use. Picking up the contrast between Martha and Mary, Mary allowed the presence of Jesus to transform her experience of time in a way that Martha resisted.

In our hyper-active culture redeeming the time is particularly about learning to sit at the Master's feet. Resisting the compulsion to work longer and harder means a gradual transformation of our priorities. In so doing we acknowledge our finitude.

Since redeeming the time is about quality rather than quantity, we can begin to do so now without any regrets about the past. One of the great prophetic promises of the Old Testament is to be found in Joel: 'I will repay you for the years the locusts have eaten' (2:25). A similar sentiment is to be found in the epilogue of the Book of Job (42:10–17). Those years cannot be replaced but their meaning can be transformed; they can be restored.

d. Becoming Christlike

However, the pervasive effects of human sinfulness mean that redeeming our time is out of our hands: it is not something we can achieve by our own unaided efforts. On the contrary, the initiative is with God. Our response is, in theological terms, repentance: a conscious turning-around and walking in a different direction, a re-alignment of our will with that of God.

A favourite metaphor for that re-alignment has been the imitation of Christ. It is rooted in Jesus' own challenge to us: 'If anyone would come after me, he must deny himself and take up his cross and follow me' (Mark 8:34). Its goal is maturity in Christ or, as Paul puts it, 'attaining to the whole measure of the fullness of Christ' (Eph. 4:13).

This growing up into the fullness of Christ is about the development of an alternative lifestyle, not about adhering to rules, or pursuing particular spiritual exercises or programmes. Such Christian discipleship can be pursued at an individual level but, more importantly, it is part of the mission of the Church as a whole.

e. Creative stewardship of time

Our situation is such that any discussion of the stewardship of time must begin with its *conservation*. We live in a world of unprecedented busyness: not even Imperial Rome could compare with the bustle of any of our big cities today (though it was a Roman who first quipped that his contemporaries died from lack of sleep).

Robert Banks reminds us that 'Unlike first-century Christians, who lived in a less pressured world and had to be exhorted to use their spare time responsibly, many Christians today need first to create free time so that they can actually have something to put to good use or "redeem".'[4] This is one of the points at which the techniques of time management can be of real assistance. They enable us to claw back free time from its despoilers, from the structural and personal pressures which tempt us to pollute our timescape.

Positively, the creative stewardship of time will be about improving the quality of our time. Banks seems to suggest that what we redeem is our free time. In later chapters we shall argue that all aspects of our experience of time can be redeemed.

But improving the quality of our time is not an exercise in self-improvement. It is about offering our time back to God and about being open to what God wants us to do with our time. The American author, Pat King, cites an example from her own experience. She and her husband decided to visit a sale at a shopping centre on their way to a late evening church meeting. When they arrived they discovered that they had come on the wrong night:

> After a moment's shock it dawned on us both that there must be a reason for it. We sat in the car and asked, 'What is it, Lord? What are we supposed to do? Who are we supposed to see?' We were both positive God wouldn't let us waste two and a half hours.[5]

After a few minutes of prayer, the same name occurred to both of them. They arrived unannounced to discover that the person they had thought of was in the middle of a crisis of faith. Because they were open to God's leadings, they were in the right place at the right time and able to help someone work through her difficulties.

Offering our time back to God brings us to worship. In worship our time is fulfilled by being caught up into God's time or heavenly time. Sadly many of us seem unwilling to give our time back to God in this way. Instead the clock is allowed to dominate church services and private devotions.

Striking exceptions to this trend are the Orthodox churches and some Charismatic fellowships. In the Orthodox tradition worship begins as and when the people have gathered and the liturgy proceeds at its own pace regardless of the passage of time outside (in some cases several hours). Charismatic fellowships may start more or less at a stated time but thereafter there is a similar freedom from the inexorable ticking of the clock.

6. Exercises

a. Martha or Mary?

Take some time to read through Luke 10:38–42 reflectively. In particular, consider the contrast between Mary and Martha. With which of the sisters do you identify more closely? Ask yourself how, in the coming week, you can take one practical step to be more like Mary and less like Martha.

b. Earthed or 'heavened'?

Os Guinness makes the following comment about busy Christians:

> With pressures and priorities like theirs, the last thing they can afford is to be 'lost in wonder, love, and praise'. Their minds as well as their watches are synchronised with 'the real world'. Securely earthed in day-to-day life, not for a moment are they in danger of being 'heavened'. Worship in any depth is negated.[6]

To what extent is this your experience of Christian worship? Think of three or four practical steps you could take to synchronize your heart, soul, mind and strength with God's time in worship. Now put them into practice!

3

How Do We Use Our Time?

> A child was taken to see a sculptor at work. He watched him wielding the hammer and chisel and the chips of stone flying this way and that. But he could see no recognizable shape, because work on this particular block of stone had only just begun.
>
> A few weeks later he was taken to the workshop again. The artist showed him the completed sculpture. The child stared in amazement: 'How did you know there was a lion in there?'[1]

All creative activity begins with a knowledge of the available materials. The sculptor knew each of his tools and its limitations. He also knew the block of stone: limestone must be treated like this, marble like that; 'I must watch out for that flaw just there.' The end result is a creative synthesis of the material's potential and the artist's vision.

The same is true of our creative stewardship of time. It begins with knowledge: of how we actually use our time, of how much time we have at our disposal, of what techniques are available to manage it better. But, like the stone and the tools, these are only the preliminaries. What matters is how we use the materials to give reality to our vision.

HOW DO WE USE OUR TIME?

THE PERILS OF NEGLECTED TIME

a. Jumbled priorities

> We have left undone those things we ought to have done,
> And we have done those things which we ought not to have done,
> And there is no health in us.

Originally these words referred to sins of omission and commission. However, most of us will, at one time or another, have felt like saying this in relation to our daily life.

In a society as complex as ours, confusion of priorities is widespread. Establishing clear priorities and pursuing them is no easy task but the results of failure are only too well known. Disorganization is a common symptom: the desk/workbench/kitchen becomes a clutter, the car is neglected, appointments are forgotten, deadlines are missed.

Confusion over priorities also leads to frustration: we seem unable to make headway with the important things because we are struggling to keep our heads above a rising tide of trivia. This can easily spill over into anxiety or guilt. We worry that we are not getting the important things done. We feel guilty that we are not glorifying God. Those unmet targets (the overflowing pending tray; the ever-increasing list of urgent household chores) may also lead to a sense of oppression. They hang over our heads like a sword of Damocles, distracting us and effectively making it still more difficult for us to get them done.

How do we get into such a state? One common reason is that we have allowed the urgent to crowd out the important. Those of us with busy lifestyles are particularly prone to this problem. If we have a reasonable amount of unplanned time, we can accommodate some unexpected or urgent demands without undue stress. However, if we are already living on a tight schedule, meeting urgent requests can easily lead to the indefinite postponement of important but non-urgent activities.

b. Over-commitment

Closely related to confusion of priorities is the temptation to over-commit ourselves. With so many people making so many quite legitimate demands on our time, it is very easy to say 'yes' too often. There are many reasons why individuals bite off more than they can chew. Here are some of the most common.

(i) Over-estimating

Over-commitment may stem from an unrealistic view of what we can achieve. Such lack of realism may be due to short-sightedness: we simply have not kept track of existing commitments.

However, it may arise from a failure to recognize or respect our creaturely limitations. We were created to inhabit a timescape structured by daily, weekly and seasonal rhythms of work and rest. The wilful rejection of those patterns in favour of some unrealistic schedule of our own making is tantamount to a declaration of human autonomy (the primordial sin recorded in Genesis 3).

(ii) Seeking to please

Another common reason for saying 'yes' when we ought to say 'no' is a desire to please or placate the other person. We may know from experience that he or she will meet our refusal with anger or a show of disappointment. Rather than face such consequences we may be tempted to say 'yes' and find some way of coping with the resultant over-commitment.

(iii) The fallacy of indispensability

It is very tempting to imagine oneself as a white knight riding to the rescue. Thus we may over-commit ourselves because of the sin of pride.

People often play on our pride when trying to persuade us to do something: 'We really need *your* contribution', 'You're the only person I can trust to do it properly', 'We can't do it without you', 'If you don't play the piano (lead the prayers, preach the sermon, etc) the morning service will be a flop', 'If you can't do it, we shall have to cancel the event'.

Sometimes we do this to ourselves. For example, we may be conscious that something is not being done and no-one else seems particularly bothered. In such circumstances we may well reason thus: 'Somebody has to do something. Nobody else seems likely to take it up. Therefore I had better do it myself.'

(iv) Guilt/sense of duty

Instead of pride these arguments may evoke guilt. Even if you are not flattered by a line like 'We can't do it without you', it may have the effect of making you feel guilty about saying 'no'.

Unfortunately such manipulation of our feelings is only too common in Christian organizations. Some tele-evangelists are notorious masters of this art. But many others use guilt as a way of drumming up support for particular causes. Contrast this with the honesty of the Anglican priest who warned a friend of ours against inner-city ministry: 'Don't come to the inner city unless you are certain God is calling you. We don't have any use for middle-class guilt trips.'

Sometimes our guilt may be due to a distorted understanding of God. Gerard Hughes describes how one person became aware of this drive:

> One day he had been imagining the marriage feast at Cana. He had a vivid imagination and had seen tables heaped with food set out beneath a blue sky. The guests were dancing and it was a scene of great merriment. 'Did you see Christ?' I asked. 'Yes,' he said, 'Christ was sitting upright on a straight-backed chair, clothed in a white robe, a staff in his hand, a crown of thorns on his head, looking disapproving.' . . . this image of Christ revealed much to him about his basic image of God and of Christ which had been hidden from him earlier. . . . As he reflected on this image of the disapproving Christ, he began to understand many things in his own life. He saw a Christ who disapproved of merriment, who demanded an unceasing application to 'good works', a tyran-

nical Christ who did not permit the simple pleasures of life. He began to realize that he had never allowed himself to admit the truth that he really experienced no joy in his multiple commitments to good works. He felt constantly guilty and driven by an inexorable God.[2]

How much of our Christian activism is the result of a guilt trip (middle-class or otherwise) or an attempt to placate an angry God?

(v) Action junkies
Some people simply can't bear to miss out. They need to be where the action is.

This may be a factor of their personality. Extraverts find that the outer world of things and events and relationships excites and energizes them. They may throw themselves into all kinds of activities for the sake of the 'buzz' that they get.

Alternatively, obsessive activism may be the result of a poor self-image. Some people use activities as a way of establishing their self-worth.

THE IMPORTANCE OF SELF-AWARENESS

How many hours a week do you spend on eating? Watching television? With family or friends? Engaged in household chores (including gardening, do-it-yourself, car maintenance, personal accounts, etc)? Church-related activities? With non-Christian friends or acquaintances? In travel? In actual work?

Genuine change can only begin from where you actually are. In order to improve the quality of your time, you must first know how you currently use it. Thus most time management courses begin with exercises which enable participants to draw up an inventory of their time use (see Exercise (a) at the end of the chapter).

In fact, this is also a common sticking point. Individuals may resist the idea of drawing up such an inventory. They may object to adding one more activity to an already crowded schedule: 'I'm already tight for time. You can't really expect me to give up a quarter of an hour a day simply to record the fact that I'm very busy!' To that we reply, 'Yes. If you genuinely want to be less busy, more effective, and feel more fulfilled.' The truth is that many of those who object to keeping a time inventory are secretly afraid of what it might reveal.

A good time log enables you to see what proportion of your time is devoted to family, the Church, the golf club, etc. It can also be very revealing of your attitudes to a variety of everyday activities since how you define 'important' depends very much on your perspective. For a workaholic, anything which is not related to work is unimportant. Thus watching your son play football might be classified as unimportant. Since watching a school football match could hardly be called urgent, this would be consigned to the category of trivia by a workaholic. However, a different perspective may result in a very different assessment: watching your son play football is an opportunity to relax (this is good in itself), it strengthens your relationship with your son (unless perhaps you are hyper-critical of his performance!) and it may be an opportunity to develop personal relationships with other parents. Thus, on at least three counts, the same activity may be seen as important when viewed from a different perspective.

The log provides you with a snapshot of your time use over what is (hopefully) a representative time-scale. However, it is unrealistic for most people to log their time use on a permanent basis. Thus the time log is not very helpful for spotting the longer-term patterns. It is unlikely, for example, to reveal any gradual changes in the amount of sleep you have. An alternative approach suitable for highlighting such longer-term changes is to keep a personal journal.

FIRST STEPS IN TIME CONSERVATION

a. Clarifying priorities

Knowing what things, activities, relationships, etc. are most important to you is probably the biggest single time saver you could have. If you have a clear idea of what is really important you will be in a much better position to resist the threat of the merely urgent.

(i) Jesus' priorities
Throughout the Gospels Jesus showed a clear sense of priorities. He was able to distinguish between the important and the urgent. What could have been more urgent than the message from Martha and Mary that their brother Lazarus was sick (John 11:3)? It was urgent, but, from Jesus' perspective, there was something more important.

Only someone who was able to distinguish the important from the urgent could have said, 'I have brought you glory ... by completing the work you gave me to do' (John 17:4). He knew that God the Father had not sent him to fulfil all the unsatisfied needs around him. He was never too busy to heal or teach those who came to him but, amidst the busyness, he never lost sight of what he had been called to do. Thus he was able to keep the urgent in perspective and was able to resist inappropriate demands upon his time and resources (e.g., John 7:6).

(ii) Singleness of purpose
Jesus knew what his calling was and he advised his disciples to have a similar singleness of purpose: 'seek first his kingdom and his righteousness, and all these things will be given to you as well' (Matt. 6:33).

'All these things' surely includes the time needed to do all that God wants of us. Clarity about God's will for our lives is an important weapon in overcoming the tyranny of the clock.

In the world, dedication to a single purpose is often a key to success. Luciano Pavarotti, like many professional musicians, is an example of dedication. As a teenager he was torn between his mother's desire that he should become a teacher and his father's wish that he should sing. After graduation he was told, 'if you try to sit on two chairs, you will fall between them. For life, you must choose one chair'.[3] We all know what choice Pavarotti made.

Such dedication is built upon a knowledge of our gifts and limitations (and, in the case of Christians, God's call). It recognizes the wisdom of Eleanor Farjeon's poem:

> There isn't time, there isn't time
> To do the things I want to do –
> With all the mountain tops to climb,
> And all the woods to wander through,
> And all the seas to sail upon,
> And everywhere there is to go,
> And all the people, every one,
> Who live upon the earth to know.
> There's only time, there's only time
> To know a few, to do a few,
> And then sit down and make a rhyme,
> About the rest I want to do.[4]

(iii) Evaluation of time

Time management experts emphasize the importance of regular reflection on your priorities and direction. Similarly within Christianity there is a strong tradition of taking time to discern what God is saying. St Paul spent some time in the desert preparing in solitude for his mission. Similarly, Augustine took a lengthy sabbatical shortly after his conversion to Christianity.

In addition to sabbaticals, regular retreats enable us to spend extended time before God seeking to discern his will for our lives. Unfortunately, the world's spirit of busyness has so penetrated the Church that many Christians today neglect this waiting before the Lord which should actually characterize our behaviour.

(iv) Prayerful prioritizing

Another favourite of time management is the regular preparation of 'to do' lists. By jotting down everything you need to do today (or tomorrow), you can create a checklist which will help prevent your being side-tracked during the day. Items can be grouped together for greater efficiency (e.g., it makes sense to block phone calls together). Some people may find that a weekly 'to do' list suits them better than a daily one.

Having listed what needs to be done, time management advises that each item be given a priority rating. A simple system is to mark each item on a three point scale: A (must be done today), B (try to do today), C (do, if time permits).

There is no reason why such prioritizing should not be done in the context of daily prayer. The 'to do' list clearly lays out what you think you ought to do during the day. Taking time to pray over your list allows you to refer it back to God. Such prayer is a recognition of your dependence upon God and of God's involvement in all your activities. Thus, as you pray over your 'to do' list, you may find that your attitude to these activities changes: the tiresome chore may become something that you can do for the glory of God, you may find that you want to do something differently (or not at all), you may 'recall' other items to add to the list.

Such waiting upon the Lord is a great help in distinguishing between the genuinely important and the merely urgent. By recalling the centrality of God in everything it also enables us to maintain our sense of direction.

Of course, these comments do not just apply to lists of things we have to do. We might usefully pray about our choice of reading matter, or television viewing, or meetings, or relationships. Prayer plays a vital part in helping us to distinguish between the central and peripheral in our lives.

b. Identifying time-wasters

If you have been honest in your keeping of a time inventory for a week or two, you will begin to see the areas where you waste time. You will be able to produce your own personal list of time wasters by noting the occasions on which you have devoted what you consider to be excessive time to non-urgent, unimportant items.

Here are a few common time wasters to compare with your own personal list.

(i) Television

Television has come to dominate leisure hours in the western world. A decade ago it already accounted for nearly half the leisure hours in North America. Its influence has certainly not diminished since then, and other western countries have been rapidly catching up with the USA in their viewing habits.

This is not to imply that television is necessarily bad. It is possible to control its use by the ruthless application of a video recorder. Nevertheless it does account for a major proportion of time use in the western world and may well account for a disproportionate amount of our leisure time.

(ii) Travel

This is often taken for granted but it can be a major drain on our time. Today we can travel faster than ever before but ironically this has not significantly reduced the average amount of time taken in getting from home to work. Thus it may be worth taking travel time into account when making decisions about job changes (or schools).

It is also a good idea to ask whether you could make better use of your time by choosing an alternative form of transport. When travelling alone we tend to go by train rather than car: it allows reading time and is less stressful than a long car journey. On the other hand, we prefer the car when travelling as a family: one of us will often read aloud while the other drives.

(iii) The telephone

It is now possible to pick up a phone and, in a matter of seconds, be speaking to someone in Canada or New Zealand. However, what the telephone offers in terms of ease of communications has to be offset against its tendency to encourage superficiality. Because it allows us to maintain a wide circle of shallow acquaintances, it may actually have an erosive effect on deep personal relationships. And, of course, possession of a telephone makes us more available.

Like the television the answer is probably responsible use rather than abandonment of the telephone. We may choose not to rely on the telephone as a way of maintaining relationships. We may reduce our availability by taking the phone off the hook or investing in an answer machine.

(iv) Looking for lost property

Citing his own personal experience, Sir Fred Catherwood warns that our acquisitive lifestyle encourages us to live with an ever-increasing clutter which only serves to frustrate us whenever we have to find something.[5]

This is not a facetious suggestion. In the world of work, looking for lost property may be translated into time wasted because of inadequate or inappropriate filing systems. Most of us will at one time or another have experienced the frustration of being told by a harassed clerk that they can't deal with our complaint/enquiry/case because they are unable to find the relevant file.

How often have you wasted ten or fifteen minutes looking for the car keys? Or the right screwdriver for that odd-job? Or a sock to match the odd one which your daughter insists she must wear with this outfit? Or your cuff-links? Or that tax return you meant to fill in last month?

Catherwood recommends tidiness. A more radical possibility would be to question whether the clutter is really necessary. Given contemporary environmental concerns, the ancient Christian virtue of simplicity may be worth reviving.

(v) Rushing

In our hyper-active society, there is continual pressure to hurry up, to get the job done quickly. However, cutting corners is not an effective strategy for conserving time.

Trying to do things too quickly increases the probability of making a mistake. What you gain now may lead to considerable waste of time and money later when you have to put it right. In some cases, such bodging may actually be life-threatening. As one of Tolkien's Hobbits put it, 'Short cuts make for long delays.' More subtly, rushing involves a continual over-riding of natural rhythms. This in turn increases our levels of stress and fatigue.

(vi) Procrastination

According to the old proverb, 'A stitch in time saves nine.' However, we are often tempted to put off a job, particularly an unpleasant one (e.g., filling in tax returns or making that difficult phone call). As the proverb suggests, jobs which are left in this way tend to grow in difficulty. Ignoring that small patch of dry rot may result in large bills and massive upheavals later on when the need for repairs becomes urgent. But even if this is not the case, the very accumulation of jobs on your 'to do' list may become oppressive. As we noted earlier this sense of oppression is one of the factors which exacerbates contemporary time pressures.

c. The importance of planning

Planning and priorities are closely related. When you have a clear idea of what is most important, of what God is calling you to do, the next step is to plan. It is essential to keep ahead of those who would gladly fill your timetable with their priorities. This can be achieved most easily by blocking out time for your own priorities as soon as you get your new calendar, diary or appointment book. In this way, when people make demands upon your time, you can honestly say, 'I'm sorry, I already have an appointment then.'

You may find it helpful to make time for your family, or for holidays, or retreats, or prayer, or study in this way. A friend of ours recently told us that he has no free weekends for the next eighteen months. This is not because he is overcommitted but because he has already planned that far ahead and made sure that he has ample time for his family and God.

(i) Quenching the Spirit?
Some people may object that such planning quenches the Spirit, perhaps citing James' warning against overconfident planning (Jas. 4:13–16). However, this surely refers to planning which ignores God. Our plans may indeed become idols. They may reflect a sinful desire to be in control of our lives to the exclusion of God. But this need not be the case.

On the contrary, just as it is possible to engage in prayerful prioritizing so it is possible to plan prayerfully. What this means is adopting an approach to planning in which the planning takes the form of a dialogue with God. James does not, in fact, object to planning as such but the planning of which he approves always carries the proviso 'God willing' (Jas. 4:15). This is not just a pious platitude. Rather, it means recognizing that all one's plans are provisional and dependent upon God. It means placing one's plans before God at the planning stage and being prepared to find that in the process of praying over them your plans change.

(ii) Planning and personality
It is important to recognize that our attitude to planning is as much a matter of personality as of theology. Some people have a constitutional distaste of detailed plans which may be rationalized as a desire not to quench the Spirit. Others may find planning congenial and in defence of their attitude argue that planning is no more than responsible stewardship. The truth is that there are some circumstances in which planning is appropriate and others in which it is not. Imagine for example a holiday which has been planned with military precision ('On Tuesday we shall go to the beach from 10.15 to 11.45 a.m. The

children may paddle in the sea between 11.20 and 11.40....
We have ways of making you enjoy yourself!').

Our attitude to planning is part of our God-given constitution and, as such, is neither right nor wrong. However, both planners and non-planners have their own characteristic way of distorting planning: the former may become obsessive and easily omit God from their plans, while the latter may fall into an irresponsible refusal to make plans. Prayerful planning allows those of us who tend to be obsessive to let God have a say, while calling those of us who are too flexible and open-ended to take greater responsibility for our time.

(iii) Realistic planning
Prayerful planning will be realistic planning. It entails a respect for your limitations as a creature: God calls us to glorify him *as creatures*. This implies knowing your own natural rhythms and respecting your own metabolism. Realism also involves allowing for the unexpected: it is a great mistake to fill up your timetable completely. If you do so, emergencies may destroy all your careful planning.

d. Just say 'no'

Our final preliminary suggestion for time-saving is to learn to say 'no'. Many Christians find this difficult. We may even feel that saying 'no' is somehow sinful.

There are no limits to the needs around us. But we are finite creatures with clear limits to the amount of time and energy we can expend without breaking down. One aspect of the Christian virtue of humility is recognizing and admitting our natural limits. It also helps to have a clear idea of your gifts and your calling. If you know that God has called you to do X, it is easier to resist requests for you to devote yourself to Y.

One secret of avoiding over-commitment or being harassed by other people's agendas is never to commit yourself immediately. It is always legitimate to ask for time to think and pray about whether to say 'yes'. Such a breathing space helps to put requests in perspective. The other person is not there to flatter or otherwise manipulate you. It gives you time to count the cost of accepting the invitation.

For example, accepting a speaking engagement involves more than the hour or so it takes to deliver the talk. The additional cost in time and energy includes the preparation time (especially if the topic is one on which you have not spoken before), travel time to and from the venue, time to be polite to all the people who hang around and chat after the talk, and (if you are an introvert) time to hide away afterwards and recover from the impact of all those people.

Another aspect to consider is that saying 'yes' to one thing always implies saying 'no' to something else. What will be ruled out by accepting this invitation? Time set aside for relaxation? For study? For prayer? For your family?

It is well worth insisting on time to think about an urgent request before saying 'yes'.

4. Exercises

a. A simple time inventory

Take a sheet of paper and put the following headings at the top:

TIME   ACTIVITY   WHO FOR?   URGENT?   IMPORTANT?

The first two columns are self-explanatory. To save time, block the day into fifteen minute segments: the time spent on each activity can be estimated simply by marking off the appropriate number of blocks.

The third column allows you to record the people and institutions which actually take up your time.

The last two columns enable you to see how much of your time is spent responding to urgent requests, how much is given

4

Time for Yourself

Holiday time! Time for yourself *par excellence*. Or is it?

For our Summer holidays last year we went to Sidmouth in Devon. We reasoned that this provided an ideal mixture of things for all the family to do: beaches for the children, pleasant country walks and interesting places to visit for us.

It poured for most of the week. We soon found our ingenuity and patience being tested to their limits as we devised ways of keeping three bored children amused and dry. Although there were plenty of places to interest us, their capacity for walking round old churches and the like is quite limited. We even resorted to sitting on the beach in the rain in order to give the children a chance to build sandcastles and paddle in the sea. On the one dry day we headed to our favourite beach only to discover that it had been taken over for the day by a massive fund-raising entertainment for some charity. We decided to stay, in spite of the canned music, but began to doubt the wisdom of our decision when gusts of wind created a mini-sandstorm around us and a plague of wasps decided to join us for lunch!

Since we were self-catering we also had all the usual household chores (shopping, preparing meals, cleaning). By the end of the week we had come to the conclusion that, whatever else it was, this had not been a holiday for us. We also decided that, until further notice, we would regard family holidays as occasions when we give extra time to our children.

over to trivia (those items which are neither urgent nor important) and how much is actually devoted to things you consider to be important.

How long should you maintain such a log? The rule of thumb is: until you feel that you have a reliable idea of your time use. This might be anything from a week (probably the minimum for most people) to a month. People whose occupations involve significant seasonal variations (e.g., teachers or clergy) may find it necessary to sample their time use at different periods throughout the year.

b. Gethsemane

Read John 17 through meditatively. It is Jesus' last night and, in his prayer, he reflects on his own priorities and his hopes for the disciples. What priorities are apparent to you in Jesus' words? Take time to reflect on each of these. How do your own priorities compare with them? Are there any you would want to make your own? Rewrite your own list of priorities in the light of this prayer. What practical steps can you take today/this week to begin to realize these priorities?

But that raises the question of what time for ourselves would look like.

THE EROSION OF FREE TIME

In chapter 1 we explored a number of factors which have conspired to create our contemporary time famine. We have too little time to meet the demands placed upon us by our relationships, our churches, our employers and society at large. Inevitably an early casualty is time for ourselves.

But once we have met these demands (or at least found some way of keeping them at bay), what remains is not necessarily free time. We give up more free time in order to service our possessions (no small item in a society as acquisitive as ours). Fatigue also takes its toll, leaving us too tired to use our free time responsibly. If any time is left, decisions about how to use it will reduce it still further.

This lack of free time is further exacerbated by the widespread utilitarianism of our society. People can readily see the value of work. But what is the value of train spotting or stamp collecting? Is not time spent in leisure activities time wasted? The result is that in order to justify leisure time, many people seek to relate it to work. Leisure is necessary in order to make us more productive during our working hours. It is often not realized that this is a negative view of leisure and free time: it may be necessary but it is not good in itself. In fact, it is little better than sick leave.

One implication of this attitude is that anything which minimizes time spent on leisure while maintaining our productivity at work must be good. Thus the busy executive may turn his weekly round of golf or his session of squash into a business meeting. Meanwhile on the shop floor, workers on the assembly line have their ears assaulted by continuous canned music (and, under Japanese business regimes, they may be encouraged to take part in mass physical exercise).

Another implication is that leisure which does not make you better able to work is bad. Some years ago a German firm took this to its logical conclusion: they successfully sued an employee who returned from his holidays too tired to do his job efficiently!

But if leisure is too closely related to work it tends to lose its leisurely qualities. A round of golf with a business associate is not leisure, it is work.

THE IMPORTANCE OF PERSONAL RHYTHMS

This emphasis on work at the expense of free time and leisure is one of the effects of industrialization in our society. Closely related to it is the way in which the natural rhythms of life have been displaced by linear clock time. Thus a good place for beginning a consideration of time for oneself is with an exploration of the extent to which we are creatures of rhythm.

a. Physiological rhythms

When God created humankind, he created physical beings with physical needs and physical limits. However, there is a persistent Christian heresy which denies our physicality. Applied to the person of Christ it took the form of Docetism: the view that Jesus was a spiritual being rather than a physical being. In a less extreme form it can be found in the tendency to emphasize Jesus' divinity at the expense of this humanity. Applied to ourselves, it results in an emphasis on the spiritual dimension of human nature at the expense of the physical. That this is deeply ingrained in western thought is plain from the fact that it has even found its way into some forms of New Age thinking, e.g., the slogan 'I am not a physical being on a spiritual journey but a spiritual being on a physical journey.'

According to Archbishop William Temple, 'Christianity is the most avowedly materialist of all the great religions.' This reflects a fundamental biblical truth: the fact of physical creation implies that the material universe is important to God, it is good. Applying this to our experience of time, we have already seen that God created us temporal beings. It is the divine intention that we be subject to the limits and rhythms imposed upon us by our physical nature.

(i) Activity and sleep

One of the most fundamental physiological rhythms with which we must come to terms is the need for a balance between activity and sleep. No one is certain why we need to sleep. It is undoubtedly a common feature of the animal kingdom and there are clear connections between lack of sleep and psychological disturbance: sleep deprivation has been widely used as a form of torture and manipulation, while inability to sleep is sometimes a symptom of excessive stress.

However, the actual balance of activity and sleep needed for good health appears to vary widely from person to person. One recent book on holiness suggests that we emulate the Benedictine pattern of no more than five hours sleep per night. On the other hand, Kenneth Leech makes the following comment about Hugh Maycock (one of the most remarkable spiritual directors of the twentieth century):

> At the centre of Hugh's day was sleep. 'When I wake up,' he once said, 'if I'm in my pyjamas, I know it's time to say Mass. If I'm not, I know it's time for tea.' The period between two and four in the afternoon was always reserved for sleep. He had even been known, during day conferences at Pusey House, to introduce a distinguished speaker at 2 p.m., then leave and go to bed, returning at 4 p.m. to close the session. Hugh believed that human beings were created to enjoy sleep. If they didn't how could they ever cope with eternity, with that 'endless Sabbath'? Ceaseless activity with no place for rest was, in his view, a very bad preparation for death and for heaven.[1]

Thus it is unwise to lay down strict guidelines about what is or isn't adequate sleep. This is something we must establish for ourselves.

Unfortunately many people today find their sleep is disturbed. The arbitrary nature of clock time has meant the loss of a natural pattern of activity and rest. Work pressures mean late night sessions to cope with urgent matters. If you find your sleep is disturbed or unsatisfying, it may be worth examining your bed-time routine. Our own experience has been that re-establishing a routine was very helpful. We now try to spend half an hour in silent prayer from about ten o'clock every evening. Quite apart from the spiritual benefits of prayer, that appointment with each other and with God enables us to bring other activities to a close well before bed-time. It also puts the day's activities in a divine perspective, enabling us to let go of them before bed.

(ii) Eating and fasting

Another physiological factor which is affected by our use of time is the balance between eating and abstaining. Busyness forces us to rush our meals, to make do with less nutritious fast foods and to neglect the relationships which would traditionally have been strengthened around the meal table. It may force us to eat at irregular intervals. We may be tempted to neglect proper meals altogether, simply grabbing a sandwich as we rush on to the next item on our agenda.

We may be able to get by for some considerable time on such a regime of neglect, but it is one more element of stress in an already stressful situation.

Sensible eating takes time. We need to allow time for the preparation and consumption of meals. Taking time over a meal allows it to become an island of rest in a busy lifestyle.

Remembering that we are creatures of rhythm, it is no bad thing to ensure that we try to eat at more or less the same times each day. The actual times do not matter a great deal – personal and cultural preferences play an important part here.

However, any English person who has ever visited Spain and tried to adjust to the local meal pattern (with the main meal of the day late in the evening) will know that a sudden change in eating patterns can be quite uncomfortable. Our biological clocks are quite adaptable but when the digestive system has adjusted to one pattern of meal times it takes a while to readjust to another.

(iii) Need for exercise
Here is another physiological requirement which is too easily squeezed out by a busy lifestyle. We are *physical* creatures and we cannot live healthy lives without an adequate amount of exercise. Therefore, in thinking about time for ourselves, it is essential to include time for regular exercise in the programme. This need not take more than a few minutes a day. What matters is that it must be done regularly. This entails some degree of routine in our daily lives.

(iv) Travelling and staying put
One rhythm which is often overlooked but which is increasingly important in our mobile society is the balance between travelling and staying in one place. Modern forms of transport have enabled us to transcend the physiological limits on our mobility. The average British person today probably travels further in a year than Jesus did in his entire lifetime.

Excessive travelling is a major unacknowledged source of stress. Consider the stress of commuting to work: will there be any delays? what if I'm late for work? The stress of long-distance travel is more clearly recognized with its sometimes devastating effect on our biological clock in the form of jet-lag. Then there is the impact on personal relationships caused by frequent moves in search of employment.

Once again we need to maintain some kind of balance. Those who spend much of their working time travelling may well need to spend their free time quietly in one place. Conversely those who work from home may want to spend their day off out of the home. That is certainly the case in our family: because

Diana is a parish deacon, we need to get out of the house on our day off to avoid non-urgent parish business.

b. *Psychological rhythms*

Since we have minds as well as bodies, there is a range of psychological rhythms which we need to recognize and respect. Amongst these are the functions identified by Jung in his theory of psychological types. We have discussed these in some detail in an earlier book.[2] However, it is worth noting their importance in passing.

In the form of Jungian typology developed by Elizabeth Briggs-Myers there are four complementary pairs of functions: extraversion-introversion; sensing-intuition; thinking-feeling; judging-perceiving. A normal person tends to show a preference for one term of each pair but is able to exercise every function.

Maintaining balance here means recognizing occasions when it is appropriate to make the effort to exercise the function or attitude which we do not prefer. For example, the extraversion-introversion polarity translates into a balance between sociability and the need for solitude. God created us as social animals: it is only as we relate to others (and/or they relate to us) that we become fully human. 'Amen!' shouts the extravert and plunges into a dizzy social round. However, relationships require a degree of otherness. It is very easy to lose touch with oneself in the busyness of continual company. Solitude is necessary to restore that degree of distance (something the introvert is much better at than the extravert). We need both: the extravert needs solitude, the introvert needs society. As Richard Foster has pointed out, 'we must seek out the recreating stillness of solitude if we want to be with others meaningfully. We must seek the fellowship and accountability of others if we want to be alone safely.'[3]

c. Spiritual rhythms

Just as there are physiological and psychological rhythms to our lives, so there are spiritual rhythms. These are perhaps the most difficult to perceive, not least because our culture lacks the vocabulary to express what is happening in our spiritual lives.

In relation to our experience of time it is important to note that our spiritual journey is by no means a smooth path. Misunderstanding at this point is a common source of disillusionment (particularly in an age which puts so much emphasis on instant success). Yes, there are times of blessing, times of intense spiritual experience. But the human spirit was not created to sustain such intensity permanently. Between the mountain peaks there are plains and plateaux: times of consolidation and slow growth. In this world there are also times of doubt and darkness. All of these weave together over the years to make the spiritual journey into an exciting pilgrimage rather than a dully uniform motorway trip.

d. Rhythms of clock and calendar

We come now to the variety of rhythms which most directly structure our experience of time.

(i) Daily rhythms

The cycle of day and night is perhaps the most obvious of these daily patterns. In earlier generations it would have been closely correlated with the daily rhythm of activity and rest. Today, however, clocks and artificial light have enabled us to detach one from the other. It is certainly part of our God-given freedom to be able to do this for some good reason but perhaps we have carried that liberty over into license. By and large our culture ignores the daily pattern of day and night in favour of its own much more rigid but quite arbitrary clock time.

We have already mentioned the role of meal times in providing the day with structure. In addition to these longer cycles, a number of modern commentators suggest that we operate on a ninety minute cycle throughout the day. This is reflected in the work pattern of Benedictine communities, which allows for a change of activity on this time-scale. Quite independently of this tradition, a number of teachers of study skills advocate changing activities on a forty-five or ninety minute pattern.

We also tend to have our individual preferences for different parts of the day. Some of us get off to a fast start; we are morning people, up bright and early. Others tend to peak later in the day. One extreme case is a friend of ours who seems to be at her best around midnight – the exception to prove what we have been saying perhaps!

(ii) Weekly rhythms

In addition to the daily patterns, our time is structured from week to week. Many religious traditions have a weekly holy day. More mundane matters also help to give the week its shape: weekly work patterns, regular meetings, the day the rubbish is picked up, the weekly shopping trip, the visit to the library.

(iii) Monthly rhythms

Men as well as women tend to operate on monthly biological cycles. This phenomenon lies behind the popularity of biorhythm calculators. However, such calculators tend to impose a highly deterministic slant on what is in reality quite flexible: these cycles can be altered or temporarily suppressed by illness, stress, jet-lag, drugs, etc. We need to identify and compensate for our monthly rhythms without falling into the idolatrous approach adopted by some New Agers. One way to identify monthly (or longer term) cycles is to keep a personal journal.[4]

(iv) Seasonal rhythms

The theologian George Hendry notes that

> In the agrarian society the division and pace of work are determined by the seasonal rhythm of nature. Nature sets the hours and the conditions of labor, and they are not

negotiable. In the industrial society ... The conditions, divisions, and hours of work have now to be organized, and as the industrial order becomes ever more vast and complex, these matters fall more and more under the control of bureaucracy.[5]

Modern industrial society has neglected the seasons and tries to suppress the difference between summer and winter in its planning. However we still live under the influence of those rhythms. When we worked as tutors at Durham University, we rapidly discovered that February was the low point of the year: it was the middle of the winter term and the number of cases of depression tended to peak in this month rather than during examinations.

Part of our stewardship of time will be recognizing such seasonal variations and making allowances in our planning. For example a pastor might put more time into study during the summer months and more into pastoral care during the winter months.

In addition to the changing seasons, the year is structured by a recurring pattern of family birthdays and anniversaries (this pattern is unique to each family and thus forms the basis for a strong family tradition); religious festivals and public holidays.

(v) The seasons of your life
Finally, the modern emphasis on clock time denies that different times in our lives have different qualities. The octogenarian remains at heart a twenty-five year old, frustrated that the physical limitations imposed by old age prevent him or her doing the things they might have done half a century ago.

An older wisdom recognizes that human life has its seasons. Different activities, a different balance of work and leisure, different behaviour patterns (even different attitudes) are appropriate at different periods in one's life. Shakespeare captures it in the well known lines: 'All the world's a stage, And all the men and women merely players: They have their exits and their entrances; And one man in his time plays many parts,

His acts being seven ages'.[6] Coming to terms with those changes is an essential part of our spiritual pilgrimage through this life.

Each of us passes through a range of seasons or phases between birth and death: childhood, adolescence and increasing independence, marriage and parenthood, retirement and old age. It is well worth taking some time to think about the seasons you have experienced and their different positive (and negative) qualities.

TIME FOR LEISURE

a. What is leisure?

By no means all of our non-working time qualifies as leisure. Time which is spent meeting obligations or engaged in compulsive activities is not genuine leisure time. Nor may mere absence of activity (passivity) be described as leisure. On the contrary, leisure entails a particular attitude to, or quality of time. According to the Roman Catholic theologian Josef Pieper, 'Leisure is a mental and spiritual attitude – it is not simply the result of external factors, it is not the inevitable result of spare time, a holiday, a week-end or a vacation. It is, in the first place, an attitude of mind, a condition of the soul'.[7]

This attitude might be described as receptivity: an openness to the possibilities in a situation without feeling the need to determine the outcome. Leisure is not something we can programme, or grasp. It is not dissimilar to the attitude described by C. S. Lewis in his autobiographical *Surprised by Joy*. Leisure, like joy, creeps up on you unawares in the moments when you are not consciously trying to achieve leisure. One busy mother describes the following example:

> Snow had unexpectedly fallen and the children were clamouring to go out in it. As I bundled them into boots and snow suits and related paraphernalia, our neighbour Lois, who was probably ten years older than I, appeared at the front door

pulling her Mary and Joanie on a sled. 'Pat, come out and play in the snow.'

'Me? I don't have the time.'

'Come on. You can spare the time.'

'No, besides I'm too old to play in the snow.'

'You'll look back and regret it if you don't.'

Reluctantly I bundled myself and the baby and out we went while I tried not to think of the porridge drying on the dishes still on the table. The children laughed with one another and created comical carrot and coal faces on their assorted snowmen. By lunch time we stood back and proudly admired our lumpy creations that grinned their frozen smiles at us.

... Lois was so right. I would have regretted missing that day far more than I ever regretted not scraping the porridge off the breakfast dishes.[8]

Leisure is an attitude of celebration. In times of leisure we enjoy the goodness of creation. Thus it flows naturally into worship: the best worship has the character of play rather than work. It is not surprising that one Christian writer comments, 'We are often most conscious of God during leisure occasions, all the way from an encounter with the beauty of nature to celebration of a birthday to observance of a holiday to the enjoyment of fine music.'[9]

b. Stewardship of leisure

The very character of leisure means that we cannot programme it. But we can programme *for* leisure. There are things we can do to make leisure easier to attain.

(i) Creature comforts

Some environments make it more difficult to adopt a leisurely attitude. It is not easy to relax in a schoolroom, an office or a factory: we have been conditioned to identify such environments with work rather than leisure. Some home environments are equally hard to relax in: the spotless living room, tastefully decorated with expensive ornaments in just the right places, is hardly conducive to relaxation (particularly for parents of small children). We need welcoming spaces, one or more comfortable rooms, in our homes. Or we need to find places where we can relax away from home: many people find that public parks or open spaces are conducive to leisure (for most city dwellers the contact with nature contrasts sharply with their accustomed working environments).

(ii) Creating free time

Free time is a necessary condition for leisure. A programme which permits little or no free time implies a low valuation of leisure (and contrasts sharply with the biblical pattern of regular rest days and frequent religious festivals). One way of combatting this is to plan well ahead of your colleagues. If the people around you plan their work schedules one month ahead, go for two months or more. And the first thing to put into your schedule is non-negotiable free time: time for yourself, time for your family, time for God.

The biblical pattern of work and rest suggests a minimum of one full day of rest every week. If you try to take time off every day, you should allow for the time it takes you to unwind from the pressures of work. A break of half an hour is of little value if it takes you an hour or more to relax! Similar considerations apply to the minimum useful length for a retreat or holiday, e.g., Diana finds that it takes her at least twenty-four hours to unwind properly at the beginning of a retreat.

(iii) Learn to relax

If you have difficulty unwinding after work, it may be worthwhile investigating some of the techniques for encouraging relaxation which are currently available. Of course, it is important to exercise discernment in your choice of relaxation techniques. Some have religious or philosophical overtones which are hard to reconcile with orthodox Christian belief. However Lawrence's favourite relaxation technique is quite innocuous:

it is to jump into a warm bath with his Sony Walkman and a Sibelius symphony.

(iv) Plan leisure opportunities

Leisure time cannot be programmed nor should we make the mistake of thinking that we can make such time 'productive' by our planning. But we can create opportunities for leisure/joy to take us by surprise.

Why not plan a walk in the countryside or your local public park? Take the kids to the swings. Find out whether there are any historical monuments, museums or art galleries near you. Plan a party: if the example of Jesus is anything to go by, God enjoys a good party!

If you are a parent it may be appropriate to plan something that will keep the children occupied while you enjoy some music or read a book or go for a walk. While they are young you might insist on them taking an afternoon nap. Of course that can't go on indefinitely – sooner or later they grow out of naps. One Dennis the Menace cartoon portrays him complaining to his mother: 'How come I have to take a nap when *you're* the one who's tired?' But, by then, they ought to be able to play more or less quietly and non-destructively in their rooms or in the garden.

TIME FOR SELF-DISCOVERY

An important aspect of leisure is its role in personal development. Many people today see themselves entirely in terms of their work. A more balanced approach recognizes that our leisure is equally important in helping to establish personal identity.

a. Time to dream

Once upon a time, about 130 years ago, a German chemist was confronted with a particularly difficult problem. He struggled with it for months but it resisted all his efforts. After one particularly exhausting day he fell asleep on the bus home. As he slept, he dreamt. And in his dream he saw snakes of many differing shapes and sizes. They began chasing their tails, forming an ancient alchemical symbol. Then these living rings turned into rings of carbon atoms. He awoke with the solution which had evaded him for so long.

This is a true story. The chemist's name was Friedrich Kekulé and the chemical whose structure he guessed in this way was benzene.

The dominant culture of the past century has had little time for dreams. They are dismissed as the rubbish of mental activity. Even Freud, who did so much to make dream analysis respectable, viewed them negatively.

We are too busy to listen to our dreams; too busy to ask what they might mean. As a result we are too busy to recognize an important dimension of our psychological make-up.

By extension we are also too busy to listen to God. Our neglect of dreams contrasts sharply with the biblical perspective in which dreaming dreams and seeing visions is a mark of the outpouring of the Holy Spirit (Joel 2:28, Acts 2:17).

Leisure time provides us with much-needed time to attend to our dreams. We ought to take time to listen to what our dreams are saying to us. As we listen we may discover previously hidden aspects of our own personality; we may begin to disentangle what we really desire from everything that we have been conditioned to want or need; we may also hear the still small voice of God speaking to us through our dreams.

b. Time to think

Gordon MacDonald suggests that 'the use of the mind for the purposes of growth is a necessary part of a God-pleasing lifestyle'.[10] However, there are many forces in modern society which actively seek to discourage us from thinking for ourselves. Advertising encourages us to buy this washing powder and that petrol without asking too many critical questions. The media are very quick to overload us with contradictory opinions on a bewildering variety of issues. Politicians are only too happy to use any technique to commend their opinions to us. Even religious leaders have jumped on the bandwagon and are prepared to use all the means at their disposal to make us accept their insights.

If we go with the flow we are, in effect, allowing others to do our thinking for us. We are abdicating our responsibility to love God with all our minds. Such abdication means that we allow ourselves to be dominated by the opinions of others; to be conformed to the hidden assumptions of our society. But Paul warns us, 'Do not conform any longer to the pattern of this world, but be transformed by the renewing of your mind' (Rom. 12:2).

Following Paul's advice takes time; time to think for ourselves. Leisure is essential if we are to find this time. If we allow the pace of life to erode our leisure, one of the first casualties will be time to think. Conversely, if we create time for leisure and protect it against the mind-dulling effects of the entertainment industry, we may begin to find the freedom necessary for the renewing of our minds.

c. Time to create

> Just think of all the poems that have never been written, songs composed, yarns told, films shot, cartoons drawn, interiors designed, pots thrown, crafts enjoyed, plays staged, furniture made – all for want of a little time and perseverence.[11]

Another casualty of our busyness is our creativity. Being creative takes time. Pressure of time means that we go for the easy option rather than the creative possibility; fast food rather than an adventurous meal. Lack of time results in a short-term perspective combined with a conservative outlook: we are not willing to consider novel ideas because they might take up more time than we can spare.

But creativity is a basic human capacity. Anything which suppresses our creativity, to that extent also suppresses our humanity.

Leisure time gives us the freedom to exercise our creativity. Most worthwhile pursuits take time. For example, painting is not just a matter of artistic flair. You do not have to be particularly gifted. What *is* needed is the time and the will to learn the techniques and practise them. The same is true of playing a musical instrument or taking good photographs.

d. Time to reflect

Introspection is a dirty word nowadays. It is often associated with the adjective 'morbid' and conjures up other words such as 'depressive', 'self-centred', 'narcissistic', 'self-absorbed'. In the 'real world' of tight schedules, busyness and hyper-activity, solitude and introspection have suffered the same fate as dreams. 'Don't just stand there, do something!' is the battle-cry of modern western culture.

Without leisure we lack the time to step back and put all our activity in perspective. We lose the capacity to evaluate our work. We find ourselves trapped on a treadmill of activity, running from one meeting to the next, never stopping to think, never pausing to ask, 'what does it all mean?' or 'does it matter?'

An important aspect of leisure is time to put work and daily life in that larger perspective. For the Christian, the leisure activity of reflection is open to God. As we take time to stop, we may also find that God has been whispering to us. Psalm 46:10 says, 'Be still, and know that I am God.' Josef Pieper's paraphrase of that verse is striking: 'Have leisure and know that I am God.'

5. Exercises

a. Putting dreams into reality

Most of us have unfulfilled longings; to learn to paint, to write a book, to go sky diving. Make a list of things you long to do. Choose one item which is a realistic short-term possibility and do something about it (e.g., if you long to paint, enrol in an art class).

Now choose a long-term possibility from your list. Take steps to find out what it would involve (perhaps by reading about it). Having gathered further information, can you now break it down into smaller parts? Which of these smaller parts can you act on? Again, do it!

b. Landmarks

This is an exercise to explore the seasons which have made up your life so far.

Take time to relax. When you feel ready, imagine your life as a mural spread out before you. What is your overall impression? Is it continuous, like a river, or a kaleidoscope of disjointed events?

Now focus on the most striking parts of the mural. What events or incidents seem to stand out? You may find it helpful to note down these events, using a key word or phrase to describe each one (if you like, these could be the chapter headings for the story of your life).

Each one of these items can itself become the basis for further exploration.

c. In God's hands

Read Psalm 139 slowly and meditatively. We have been considering time for self. What do these verses say to you about such time?

5

Time for Family and Friends

Gordon MacDonald recounts the following conversation with a neighbour:

> As we walk along, we talk about the plight of the contemporary man in industry. Charlie says something like this to me, 'Let's face it, Gordon; you can't easily be a success with the family and a success in the business world. Something has to go. They've offered me a top job in our company's executive management team. But do you know what that requires? A hotline telephone on my night table at home. Dinner with the company president three or four times each week. Business breakfasts every morning. Frequent plane trips all over the country. Weekend conferences at the whim of the president. You make a lot of money, and you get a lot of privileges, but the fact remains: you can't be a company man and a family man. One of them suffers. I love Joan and the kids too much; I told them to keep the job and give it to someone else.'[1]

INTRODUCTION: TIME FOR RELATIONSHIPS

a. Busyness and the poverty of our relationships

According to conventional wisdom, time is money and, for many people, seems to be in short supply. At the same time, ease of communications tempts us to maintain more relationships. Apparently the average Londoner meets more people in a week than his or her pre-industrial ancestor would have met in a lifetime!

Inevitably time is rationed – even time for our closest relationships. One result is the myth of *quality time*. The real motive behind this belief was revealed very clearly by one of the characters in the Doonesbury cartoon strip. Asked to explain what he understood by this concept he replied,

> Quality time is the kind of time you spend with your kids if you're really too pressed to give them the more traditional quantity time. By giving a child quality time, that is, highly concentrated doses of focused attention, the busy parent can shave valuable hours off the time required to impact his child's development ... It works with old people too, by the way.[2]

But such hoarding of time easily degenerates into superficiality and inattention. Visits to relatives cease to be a positive part of our leisure time. If they are not crowded out altogether by other commitments, they become 'duty visits'. Time spent meeting an obligation feels very different from time freely given to someone. Quality time may have a grudging quality about it which its victims experience as lack of concern. Because of the busyness of our culture some people go through life experiencing only superficial relationships.

But, if busyness has had this impact on our closest relationships, how much more has it affected our friendships! More than thirty years ago, C. S. Lewis argued that few of us have experienced genuine friendship. He tried to explain this in psychological and philosophical terms. In fact, most of us simply do not have time for friends. Genuine friendship is time-intensive. Most of us are so busy that we never really get to know the people we call our friends. Thus, many of us can identify with the parents of American psychiatrist M. Scott Peck:

> Had someone asked my parents whether they had friends, they would have replied, 'Do we have friends? Good gra-

cious, yes. Why, we get over a thousand Christmas cards every Christmas!' On one level that answer would have been quite correct. They led a most active social life and were widely and deservedly respected – even loved. Yet in the deepest definition of the word, I am not sure they had any friends at all. Friendly acquaintances by the drove, yes, but no truly intimate friends.[3]

b. Time for others

This reality contrasts sharply with biblical teaching about time and relationships. In Chapter 2 we suggested that, far from viewing time as a commodity, the biblical authors saw it as a gift: the gift of God to all creatures. Thus the appropriate attitude is generosity rather than hoarding. As with all of God's gifts, 'Freely you have received, freely give' (Matt. 10:8).

A biblical understanding of human relationships leads to a very similar conclusion. When God created human beings, he did not create isolated individuals. Both Genesis 1:27 and 2:18–25 speak of the creation of a basic social unit. Man alone was incomplete: the creation of humankind was the creation of a society. Furthermore, it is precisely personal relationship (exemplified by the relationship between man and woman) which is identified as the image of God in humankind (in Gen. 1:27).

But if, as this suggests, personal relationships are an essential part of what it is to be human, the contemporary pressure in favour of busyness and individualism is a dehumanizing force. If we devote our time entirely to self-fulfilment we shall, in the end, lose our true selves. The Christian understanding of persons and relationships suggests that time for others is an essential complement to time for self. Denying others that time is a denial of our own humanity.

c. Why families?

Readers may wonder why we have put families and friends together. Some will object that the family is such an important part of Christian belief that it deserves its own chapter. Others (particularly single people) may object that the word 'family' is exclusive: most people today do not live in stable traditional families.

However, both objections share the assumption that the nuclear family of husband, wife and two or three children is the 'traditional' model of family life. This is simply not the case. On the contrary, the nuclear family is a relatively recent invention of western culture.

Turning to the Bible, the Hebrew word most often translated as 'family' can also be translated as 'household' or even 'clan' (e.g., Judg. 18:11). Similarly, in the Greek of the New Testament, the word usually translated as 'family' is *oikos* or 'household' (the root of the English word 'economy'). Thus, in biblical usage, the nearest equivalent to our 'family' was a socio-economic group of indefinite size bound together by a variety of relationships. It would certainly contain married couples, parents and children. But it would also include people who were bound together in other ways: by friendship, by economic ties, etc.

Seen in this light, several students sharing a house or a group of Christians exploring community together might be seen as a family. Family life is bigger than the nuclear family. God did not intend us to live in tiny exclusive social units but in a flexible open network of personal relationships.

TABLE FELLOWSHIP

a. The focus of social life

For millennia the common meal has been the focal point of social life. Those with whom our ancestors customarily shared their food were their nearest and dearest. The camp fire was also the place where the culture would be passed on to the next generation as story-tellers and musicians entertained/educated their fellows.

The close connection between friendship and hospitality may be seen in the scandal which still clings to the violation of hospitality. Judas' betrayal of Jesus is particularly heinous because he is 'one who dips bread into the bowl with me' (Mark 14:20), i.e., he is one of those closest to Jesus. Similarly the Massacre of Glencoe is remembered as a black chapter in Scottish history because the soldiers who carried out the attack first accepted the hospitality of their victims.

The Bible shares this almost universal emphasis on the importance of table fellowship. For example, the Gospels make a point of recording the complaints that Jesus ate with outcasts and sinners. By eating with them he identified himself with them in a way that scandalized 'decent folk'. The New Testament even describes our relationship with Jesus in these terms: 'I stand at the door and knock. If anyone hears my voice and opens the door, I will come in and eat with him, and he with me' (Rev. 3:20). Similarly, the object of the Christian hope is frequently portrayed as a meal: the marriage feast of the Lamb.

The importance of eating together can also be seen in the history of Christian worship. Our Eucharist or communion service originated in the context of a common meal (1 Cor. 11:17–34). There has also been a recurring tendency, over the centuries, for groups of Christians to share common meals. Thanksgiving feasts were popular with the Puritans. Today we see it in the church supper or parish lunch.

Common meals certainly feature prominently in community life. The community of which we were members for two years has two such meals each week at which every member is expected to be present. Those meals and the social events associated with them play an important part in binding people together.

By contrast today's busy lifestyle has led to the abandonment of the leisurely common meal in favour of more 'efficient' cafeteria-style eating habits. One commentator warns that this 'habit of "grazing", in which members of a family wander into the kitchen whenever they are hungry, to re-heat processed food, and then sit down in front of the television to eat it, is a threat to the integrity of the family'.[4]

More broadly, such 'grazing' spells the demise of what has been, historically, the most important way of developing personal relationships. Conversely, we may redress the balance by putting more emphasis on eating together, whether with members of one's immediate family or with friends.

b. Practical suggestions

To begin with, we can take steps to guard against 'grazing'. It is probably unrealistic to demand that all meals be eaten together. However, in most households it should be possible to have one common meal each day, probably the evening meal. Others may find it more realistic to start with just one or two meals per week. But however frequent or infrequent these common meals, they should be important commitments for every member of the family or household (e.g., not something to be missed because of a club meeting or TV programme).

Having established a regular pattern, it must be protected against intrusions. Since ours is a clergy household, the telephone is a serious offender. What we have done is impress upon parishioners that the period between 5.00 p.m. and 7.00 p.m. each day is a family time when we do not wish to be disturbed. Having done that, we make sure our answering machine is switched on during those hours and we resist the temptation to answer when the phone does ring.

Positively, such meal times should be worth attending. With a little thought they can be turned into enjoyable occasions. After all, they are not just about ingesting the appropriate amounts of nourishment to keep the body working efficiently. Thus conversation (and guests) should be encouraged. Table decorations, special crockery and cutlery, and favourite foods all serve to underline that this is a special time. Why not look for something to celebrate? When we lived in community, the Friday evening common meal was birthday party night complete with cake and games.

Contrary to popular mythology, the Puritans were masters of the art of finding something to celebrate! They invented the American Thanksgiving Day (which, in its original form, lasted *three* days). In addition to that communal celebration, individual Puritan families would hold regular days of thanksgiving to celebrate everything from weddings to recovery from illness.

The meal table may also become the focal point for family prayers.[5] One of the strengths of Jewish religious life is that it has retained this dimension of worship.

MAKING TIME FOR EACH OTHER

a. The goal of friendship

Perhaps because friendship is relatively rare in our society, many people suppose that it is largely a matter of distraction: friends are those with whom we pursue leisure activities, with whom we amuse ourselves. But the Christian emphasis on personal relationships suggests an alternative goal, namely, mutual enrichment. A good example of such mutually enriching friendship would be the Inklings: Owen Barfield, C. S. Lewis, J. R. R. Tolkien and Charles Williams. It was during their meetings that early drafts of some of their best known works (notably *The Lord of the Rings*) were read and discussed.

However, friendship does not have to produce such results to be worthwhile. As Robert Banks points out,

> friendship does not have to issue in anything like this to have real value. Ultimately friendship is its own reward. Simply being with others whom we like and enjoy, growing together in intimacy and understanding, is more than enough. We

experience too little of these in our world today. Yet they are one of the main sources of our growth to maturity.[6]

Each of us needs fellow pilgrims with whom we journey through life. They are a source of joy and strength – such strength that C. S. Lewis was moved to describe friendship as 'almost our strongest safeguard against complete servitude'.[7]

Too often we fail to make the connection between friendship and family. The Bible, by blurring the edges of the family, suggests that they are indeed intimately related. As Christians we say that we place great importance upon the family but too often we give the lie to this by failing to make friends of family members. One way we could begin to redress the balance is to take more interest in the things that really interest them.

b. *The secret of simplicity*

What has the Christian discipline of simplicity to do with time for personal relationships? Admittedly the relationship is not direct. But we believe simplicity does have important implications for the time we are able to give to friends and family.

Outer simplicity is about detachment from material goods. Thus it is a powerful aid when it comes to disentangling ourselves from the spider's web of greed, acquisitiveness and hyperactivity which characterizes modern life. Simplifying our lifestyle brings about immediate time savings which can then be translated into time for other people. In the longer term it may also help us sit more lightly to the demands of modern life. If we have discovered that we can live a fulfilling life on a modest income, we will be better able to resist pressures to do more overtime, or take that promotion, or a second job. It may also help us cope more creatively with redundancy.

But simplicity also has to be practised in relation to our social commitments. One reason why many people find that their relationships are conducted on a fairly superficial level is simply that they spread themselves too thinly. There are so many activities and social events on offer that there is not sufficient time to devote to any particular set of relationships. This lack of time created by social busyness also affects parent-child relationships. One American mother reflecting on life in Kenya commented that, 'I now realize that in the US I did not have time or at least I did not take the time necessary to parent. And after Scouts, sports, school, church, parties, music, and camp my children did not have the time or energy to be parented'.[8]

What are we to do about this? The brutal answer is that we have a choice: we can choose to maintain a busy social schedule or we can cut back in order to make more time for deep friendships with a few people. We cannot have our cake and eat it. As with cutting back on our possessions, however, this need not be a dramatic withdrawal from public life. A more sensible approach is to list what one does regularly and ask which activities are most important. Most people should be able to achieve significant cuts in their outside activities without abandoning any real commitments.

The positive side of this process is, of course, making decisions about which friendships to cultivate.

The experience of that American mother quoted above has important implications for households in which there are children. In the light of what we have been saying, it will be one of the duties of the adult members of the household to protect children from this busyness. The pressures of modern society are such that it is quite possible for an eight year old to be involved in a bewildering rat-race of activities after school: ballet, gymnastics, karate, music lessons, Cubs and Brownies, sports clubs of all sorts, not to mention church youth groups. It is not uncommon for children of this age to have one or more such activities after school every day of the week (with more at the weekends).

Parents of two or three school-age children may find that their afternoons and evenings are taken up with ferrying children from one activity to another. This need not be time wasted. On the contrary, it may be a marvellous opportunity for conversation and closeness. For example, we found that the walk home from school was a particularly valuable time for chatting with our eldest daughter, helping her to share her worries during a difficult patch.

Our response to social pressures on our children's time has been to ration them: our eldest child is permitted to choose two weekly after-school events. A similar approach may be adopted to the endless variety of TV programmes for young people: each child is permitted to choose so many programmes per week (with the possibility of certain programmes being censored by parents).

The point of this rationing is a positive one. On the one hand, it protects children from the full effects of contemporary busyness. On the other, it forces them to decide what is really important to them. Thus it constitutes a training in making responsible choices which, hopefully, will stand them in good stead later in life.

c. Spending time together creatively

Having created time for others, what should we do with it?

In a sense the most important thing is simply to make that time available. The development of relationships requires quantity as well as quality time. This will mean giving over entire days, weekends and holidays to family members and special friends. And this time commitment cannot be a one-off: friendship requires continuing contact. There may be long periods when we do not see each other. But when we do get together, we should not be governed by the clock.

Of course time together can be enriched by a certain amount of planning. The possibilities are endless and one or two simple ideas will certainly enrich our time together. Beware of overplanning: elaborate plans may get in the way of the very relationship they were supposed to foster; they may also squeeze the fun out of the activity (e.g., by turning a visit to the museum into a purely educational activity).

There is a close relationship between creativity and fun. Spending time together creatively involves having fun together. Jumping in puddles with a child may be a more creative way of spending half an hour than making them do something 'educational'.

(i) Tradition

From time immemorial, traditions have been important in strengthening personal and social relationships. They are no less valuable today. However, they have to be used with care. Artificiality or self-consciousness in their use is likely to be self-defeating.

In fact, many time-hallowed family traditions have evolved around the meal table: the ritual of a Sabbath or Passover meal; the traditional Christmas dinner; the practice of saying 'Grace' before (or after) a meal. But it could be something as simple as 'we always used to toast muffins in front of a log fire on Sunday evenings.'

Every family or household has its own particular ways of doing things – its own particular traditions. It is well worth paying attention to these: to ensure that they are done thoughtfully. And why not invent new traditions; practices that will give your family its own unique identity?

Bedtime traditions are particularly meaningful to children. Precise details are not important. What does matter is that the routine conveys that they are loved rather than a nuisance to be bundled off to bed as rapidly as possible. In our household it is a time for reading stories together, playing games and praying together.

Every household has its own unique pattern of anniversaries and birthdays. Imposed on this will be the religious festivals associated with the religious tradition of that household and the secular holidays of school and workplace. All of these are times for building up personal relationships. Therefore some investment of time in thought and preparation for the event is well worthwhile.

(ii) The necessities of life

In a household, creative time together need not be limited to special events. One of our abiding memories of the community in which we met is of the way in which even the most mundane household chores became social events. Conversations sprang up over kitchen tables as meals were prepared; people would be arguing, or praying, or laughing together while weeding the vegetables, or cleaning the toilets, or doing the laundry for fifty people.

There is less opportunity for this in the nuclear family. But what about taking time to chat to your neighbour? Or stopping to talk to people you meet when you go shopping?

And children need not be left out. Household chores can be turned into games. How fast can we clear away the 'Lego'? Who wants to weigh out the flour? Who is going to help mix the pudding? Young children love to help. Admittedly their help can make the task take twice as long. But that does not matter if you have already decided that time with your children is as important as getting the job done.

(iii) Outings

Finally there are days out and holidays. Again some planning is helpful to ensure that there is something for everybody.

Even very young children can enjoy an art gallery or museum. The secret is not to look at too much, to find things which will capture their imagination, and to provide art materials so that they can draw whatever excites them. For example, our last visit to the National Gallery centred on Rousseau's *Tropical Storm with a Tiger*. We took paper and pencils with us and two out of our three children settled down to copy the tiger. Joanne, however, decided to perform it instead – she crawled about the gallery floor, growling!

Of course a certain amount of planning is helpful even if no children are involved. A trip to an art gallery or museum is greatly enriched if a member of the party has taken the trouble to find out a little about some of the exhibits. Similarly a visit to a site of architectural or historical importance will come to life if someone in the party knows something about what took place there: Bosworth Field is just that without some acquaintance either with the Wars of the Roses or Shakespeare's *Richard III*. And the same is true of any walk in the countryside: a little knowledge sought out in advance allows us to see things we would otherwise have overlooked (which flowers are in bloom? what birds are we likely to see? what kind of insect is that? how did those rock formations develop?).

GIVING TIME TO EACH OTHER

So far we have concentrated on spending time *with* others. However, another important aspect of resisting the temptation to hoard time, is being willing to give up your time *for* others. There are times in our lives when what we need most is to be given a break from routine. Conversely there are times when we have the freedom to enable others to take a much needed break.

For example, we might be prepared to give up some of our leisure time to go shopping, or do some gardening or handiwork for someone who is unable to do it for themselves. Or we might consider taking over the household to allow our partner to take some time off. Gordon MacDonald makes the interesting suggestion that 'we who are husbands need to ask whether or not we are creating and guarding time for our wives to read and study'.[9] But it need not be limited to time for self-improvement or, for that matter, to married couples. In this way we may be able to help a partner or close friend to find time to relax, or study, or pray, or even take a holiday. For example, some months ago we added the son of a family friend to our family for a week so that she could take advantage of the unexpected offer of a week in Turkey with her husband.

There comes a time in every household when we have to give up time for those around us. Sickness in the family demands that we give up our own interests and look after those of the invalid. Before we had children of our own we used to wonder how friends with several children managed to survive the continuous round of bugs which afflicted them every winter.

There are periods in every life when people have little time or energy to spare for family or friends. It is at times like these that we can show true friendship by stepping in and offering them some time off. The couple with a new baby might well appreciate the few hours alone together that an offer of babysitting represents. A few years ago some friends took over our home and our three children for a weekend, allowing us to have our first weekend away together since the children were born. As you can imagine, it was much appreciated! And, of course, giving time *to* the parents in this way may also be seen as time *with* the children, building up another set of friendships which may last a lifetime.

Another period when such respite would be very welcome is when people are caring for elderly parents or a disabled or sick partner.

The Christian community could do much more to support people in this way. A homegroup might come to see itself as the modern counterpart of the extended family: enjoying life together, giving time to each other. Of course, the point we are trying to make is that we *are* the Christian community. If Christian community is to be a tangible reality it has to be incarnated in our lives through such practical caring for one another.

5. Exercises

a. Who is your family?

Forget about the conventional nuclear family. Stop and ask yourself these questions.

To whom do you actually relate deeply and on a regular basis? Who would you talk to if you were made redundant?

Who would you turn to if you were told that you had cancer? Who would you put in your will? Who do you eat with regularly? With whom do you share a home?

Having identified your 'family', ask yourself how much time you spend with them. Do you feel that this is too little? about right? excessive? What practical step can you take this week to enrich your relationship with each one of your 'family' members?

b. Family retreat or quiet day

Plan a day off together to consider before God how you might strengthen your relationships? As Edith Schaeffer points out,

> There is a great need for *stopping* as a family together, praying for a whole evening, for a whole day off together, discussing, praying, asking God, 'Please show us before it is too late; what balance are we to have in our family in order to have time together before it is too late?'[10]

c. Love is . . . is not

Take some time to meditate on 1 Cor. 13:4–7. As you repeat the words in your mind, ask how they relate to your personal relationships. Does any part of the passage strike you as particularly relevant to your situation?

6

Time for the World

Michelle is married, with three young children. The two oldest are school age; the youngest is delicate and needs constant attention. To meet basic household costs, Michelle does hand-knitting of mohair sweaters at home. It can take her up to thirty-five hours to knit a complicated pattern, and she is paid £8.50 for it. That sweater then has a designer label added and is sold in the high street for an inflated price.

Michelle does not live in the Third World, she lives in Leeds. There are thousands of women like her in West Yorkshire. The Christmas decorations you bought last year may well have been made in Leeds: some of the women who assemble them are paid less than 20p per hour.

How many of us take time to see and respond to the injustices on our doorstep?

THE EROSION OF PUBLIC LIFE

We commented in Chapter 1 that the public life of our society was one of the casualties of contemporary time pressures. In recent years this has become increasingly obvious in election campaigns both in Britain and North America. There has been a noticeable shift in emphasis from issues to personalities; from reasoned arguments to image and slogans.

This was highlighted by one commentator on the 1992 American presidential elections. He noted that during the campaign

George Bush made about five hundred speeches focusing on the character of Bill Clinton but only two focusing on the state of the economy!

While it is by no means the only factor, sheer lack of time has certainly contributed to this degeneration in our political life. The move from a debating style (which demands considerable time both of politicians and the electorate) to an advertizing campaign (which influences people without demanding anything like the same investment of time and energy) reflects the fact that many people simply do not have time to listen to the arguments and come to a reasoned conclusion.

The sheer quantity of public information available and the rate with which it changes forces us to narrow our focus. The detail available to us makes the prediction of trends more difficult: we simply cannot see the wood for the trees. As a result some decision-makers become less willing to take risks; they stick with known policies even when it is recognized that they don't work! Others may be tempted to adopt the 'quick and dirty' approach, supporting the most obvious or attractive policy without considering its longer-term implications. Neither strategy seems calculated to ensure the long-term health of our society.

In short, we simply do not have time to be good citizens. Many of us find that we have no time to attend to the issues. And many of those who do manage to keep up with the issues find that they have no time to exert influence on the decision-makers. How many people reading this chapter have ever written a letter to their MP?

One result of lack of time in this sphere is that political influence tends to become the preserve of enthusiasts, pressure groups and professional lobbyists.

a. No time for strangers

But it is not just at the level of local or national politics that time pressures take their toll. It is also very obvious at a personal level. Many of us have no time for strangers – especially needy strangers. Henri Nouwen comments that 'Our society seems to be increasingly full of fearful, defensive, aggressive people anxiously clinging to their property and inclined to look at their surrounding world with suspicion, always expecting an enemy to suddenly appear, intrude, and do harm.'[1] One reason for this suspicion of strangers is that we do not have time to treat them as fellow human beings. Recognizing the other as a person entails being prepared to take the time to get to know them.

Take the Parable of the Good Samaritan (Luke 10:25–37). The priest in the story may have had a good reason for not stopping: 'A man lying by the roadside! He looks in a bad way. What should I do? I suppose I ought to help. But wait, what if he's already dead? Look at all that blood. If I touch him I shall make myself unclean. And I'm due to serve in the Temple tomorrow. I would miss my turn. Surely my duty to God takes priority. And this is a busy road. Someone else will pass by soon. A few minutes won't make any difference to him.' He may simply not have had time to spare for the needy stranger.

Responding to a cry for help takes time. In our society with its time pressures it is easier to pass by on the other side. How often have we hurried past the beggar or the drunkard lying in the street? How often have we deflected the cry for help with a few pence, or a few pounds, or a credit card donation?

But what are we saying if we admit that we have no time for strangers? It implies that we have no time for Christian witness. Worse, it implies that, in spite of all our prayers, we have no time for God.

b. *The privatization of personal life*

This lack of time for strangers or for political life is not merely a personal problem. It is, in important measure, a function of the way modern society is structured.

One of the unquestioned assumptions which has shaped

modern society is that there is a sharp distinction between the public and the private worlds. The public realm is the realm of facts and objectivity. The private realm is the appropriate place for opinions, religious faith and personal relationships. This distinction has been reinforced in a number of ways. On an intellectual level it is underpinned by a sharp distinction between facts and values: scientific 'facts' belong to the realm of public truth whereas morality, aesthetics and faith have been relegated to the realm of private opinion. On an economic level it has been reinforced by the almost complete divorce between work and home. Prior to the industrial revolution, home life could not be separated from public life because for many people the home was the work place. Commenting on the effects of divorcing work from the home, Bishop Lesslie Newbigin notes that,

> The home is no longer the place of work, and the family is no longer the working unit. The way is opened for a deep divide between the public world of work, of exchange, of economics, and the private world that is withdrawn from the world of work and remains under another vision of how things are. In the public world the workers in the factory are related to each other anonymously as units in a mechanical process. They are replaceable parts. They may not even know each other's names. In the home people are known to one another as irreplaceable persons, and their mutual understanding as persons is what constitutes the home.[2]

That dichotomy between public and private creates a barrier between us and strangers; a barrier that is reinforced by the advice we give to our children: 'Don't talk to strangers!' Strangers inhabit the public realm: the realm of impersonality. We are expected to relate to them impersonally. As a result we may feel profoundly uncomfortable if the stranger sitting next to us on the bus or train tries to strike up a conversation. Steve Turner has captured this unease in a poem simply entitled

'Stranger' which reflects on the fact that each one of us is a stranger. It concludes with the lines,

> It's strange
> being a stranger.
> There seems little chance
> of breaking out.
> Or if I was to,
> it would only confirm
> my strangeness.[3]

The family, far from being the basic unit of society, has been transformed into a barrier against society. This is not only true of relationships with strangers. It has also been noted as one of the factors behind the degeneration in political involvement:

> The notion of family privacy, now so taken for granted, may be seen as a relatively recent development, stemming from the requirements of a society switching its main energies into the production of goods and services. The result was a loss of contact with formal political debate, which then also became more specialized.[4]

What has this to do with time? The point is simply that the structures within which we live do not allow us time for strangers or for political engagement. Nor is it merely the way industry is structured that has this effect – basic social institutions, like the nuclear family, are also implicated.

TIME FOR STRANGERS

Donald Nicholl describes his arrival at Heathrow Airport in a state of 'frozen despair' several hours after leaving his father's deathbed. It was early in the morning and the place was deserted. He was completely disorientated. Then he spotted a young woman in uniform:

I moved over to my left to intercept her, and I asked her if she knew where I was supposed to go in order to secure a stand-by place on a Pam-Am flight to San Francisco. Though she was clearly in a hurry she stopped to listen to me, and then looked kindly at me as she answered that she was sorry but she didn't know.

And then something happened. Whether it was some note of sadness in my voice that she picked up or whether she saw something in my face that moved her – whatever it was, she had been touched. Perhaps that is why she in turn touched my sleeve and said, 'Wait a minute, my love. I think I may be able to help you. Please come with me.' And at that she led me across the hall towards a window on which she tapped. Soon a man appeared to whom she explained my need, and he straightaway assured me that if I were to wait outside his window for a quarter of an hour he would assign me a place on the flight to San Francisco.

... To an outsider that casual encounter on a deserted Heathrow between an unusually tall, bearded man wearing a duffle coat and a dumpy woman airport worker could hardly have seemed of any importance in the life of either the man or the woman. They had never met before and they have never met since ...

But the man, myself, will never forget how his numbed heart was melted by the warmth in the woman's voice when, though a total stranger to him, she said, 'my love'. I have wondered since if she often says 'my love' to total strangers or whether it was the Spirit of God which inspired her to do so that winter morning.[5]

a. Hospitality in the Bible

It is proverbial that 'a man's house is his castle'. But, far from being a castle, the Bible presents the home as a place of hospitality. Righteousness is expressed by showing practical love to the stranger and alien, to widows and orphans, to the poor and oppressed.

This is true of the Old Testament law: 'you are to love those who are aliens, for you yourselves were aliens in Egypt' (Deut. 10:19; cf. Lev. 19:34). Even when the Israelites were again exiles (this time in Babylon), God challenges them 'to share your food with the hungry and to provide the poor wanderer with shelter' (Isa. 58:7).

A similar challenge is to be found in the New Testament. Jesus identifies the righteous thus, 'I was hungry and you gave me something to eat, I was thirsty and you gave me something to drink, I was a stranger and you invited me in' (Matt. 25:35). When did I do anything for you, Lord? My daughter, when you helped that stranger find the right window at Heathrow, I was that stranger. When you stayed up half the night, sobering up a drunk student, I was that student. When you sat with that AIDS victim, you sat with me. 'Whatever you did for one of the least of these brothers of mine, you did for me' (Matt. 25:40). And the writer of the Letter to the Hebrews advises his readers, 'Do not forget to entertain strangers, for by so doing some people have entertained angels without knowing it' (Heb. 13:2).

Nor is the Bible content with teaching about the importance of hospitality. It offers many practical examples. Abraham welcomes the strangers who approach him at the Oaks of Mamre only to find that he has been entertaining God (Gen. 18:2ff). Lot, whom many modern readers would be tempted to write off, is singled out as righteous and demonstrates his righteousness by offering the messengers of God his hospitality and protection (Gen. 19:1–3). The widow of Zarephath finds blessing in the hospitality she extends to Elijah (1 Kings 17:10–24) and a similar story is told of hospitality extended to his successor, Elisha (2 Kings 4:8–37). Examples from the New Testament include the disciples on the road to Emmaus, who invite in the stranger only to discover that he is the risen Lord (Luke

24:13–35); and Lydia who opened her home to Paul and his companions (Acts 16:15).

Far from being a potential enemy, a threat or a danger the stranger in the Bible is the particular object of God's love. In Deuteronomy we are told, 'the Lord your God is God of gods and Lord of lords, the great God, mighty and awesome, who shows no partiality and accepts no bribes. He defends the cause of the fatherless and the widow, and loves the alien, giving him food and clothing' (Deut. 10:17ff).

b. Hospitality as reconciliation

The God and Father of our Lord Jesus Christ is a God who loves the stranger. He actively seeks to reconcile those who have become estranged from him.

Thus offering hospitality to strangers may be seen as an act of reconciliation. In our society the stranger is a threat. Consider the way we treat those who are displaced by famine or war. So long as they keep well away from our shores, they are regarded as refugees and we are happy to send them relief. However, if they should happen to arrive in our backyard they become 'economic migrants': a threat to our jobs, our property and even our culture.

The reconciling power of hospitality transforms the stranger into a guest. In the process the potential enemy may be transformed into a friend. How often have we judged someone on first sight? Their clothes or their hairstyle fill us with suspicion. Will they remember to wipe their shoes on the doormat? Will they pocket something small but valuable if we leave them alone in our sitting room? And how often have we discovered our fears to be unfounded after we have taken the trouble to get to know them as persons?

Hospitality overcomes the stereotypes with which we set ourselves apart from strangers. He is no longer that 'copper'; she is no longer that New Ager. Instead she becomes Mary Jones who plays the piano beautifully, or bakes marvellous cakes, or is passionately concerned about social justice. He becomes Joe Smith who gardens, or supports Manchester United, or writes poetry when he is off-duty.

As the enmity and stereotypes evaporate what takes their place is a personal relationship: a relationship of equality in which we discover new things about ourselves as well as about our guest. Thus the stranger may be an angel incognito: a messenger of God who brings to our attention things which may help us to grow in our relationship with God.

Hospitality may be seen as an acted parable of God's grace. As we reach out to strangers in love and hospitality we reflect something of the grace of the God who reaches out to those who are estranged. The stranger symbolizes our exile. But at the same time the stranger stands in the place of God. In offering hospitality to the stranger we are offering hospitality to God.

c. Giving time to strangers

But just what does hospitality involve? Henri Nouwen suggests that one of the most important features of hospitality is that we give strangers space (or, more accurately, time), not emptiness but a friendly place

> where strangers can enter and discover themselves as created free; free to sing their own songs, speak their own languages, dance their own dances; free also to leave and follow their own vocations. Hospitality is not a subtle invitation to adopt the lifestyle of the host, but the gift of a chance for the guest to find his own.[6]

Hospitality is, first of all, giving time to strangers. A bed for the night and a meal are actually less important than this gift of time. It is possible to give the material gifts of food, clothing and shelter without giving any hospitality at all. Indeed, in our time-starved society it is not uncommon for material goods to become a poor substitute for the gift of time even within families.

Giving time to others so that they can be themselves is not an easy option. Nature abhors a vacuum and so does the sinful human ego. We find it very hard to resist the temptation to fill any space/time that is created with ourselves, our own concerns and interests. We chatter away and at the end of the evening congratulate ourselves on being hospitable when, in fact, we are no closer to our guest than when they first entered our house.

Thus hospitality demands an attitude of receptivity and acceptance. It means caring enough about the other to want to know who they are. It means giving them time to tell their story.

d. Hospitality as confrontation in love

The fact that we do not try to impose our views on the stranger/guest does not imply that we must be entirely neutral in our hospitality. On the contrary, neutrality may be a denial of genuine hospitality. Genuine hospitality is about giving time to the other so that a personal relationship may develop. Neutrality is more like giving the stranger a front-door key and leaving them to get on with it. Henri Nouwen suggests that

> An empty house is not a hospitable house. In fact, it quickly becomes a ghost house, making the stranger feel uncomfortable ... When we want to be really hospitable we not only have to receive strangers but also to confront them by an unambiguous presence, not hiding ourselves behind neutrality but showing our ideas, opinions and life style clearly and distinctly.[7]

Thus Christian hospitality is a kind of dialogue. The controlling feature is an unconditional love which accepts and affirms the guest regardless of creed, colour, social background or sex. But alongside that receptivity there is an element of confrontation:

hospitality means that we do not hide who we are or what we believe.

Restoring this kind of hospitality to a central place in Christian family life would be an important step in breaking out of the privatized ghetto of the modern family. John Finney's recent survey of factors involved in coming to Christian belief suggests that it might also be an important reaffirmation of the mission to which God calls all Christians.[8]

Clearly, for most of us, offering hospitality to strangers is not something we can easily programme into our weekly schedule. However, we can learn to be more sensitive to God-given opportunities to entertain strangers/angels. In large measure such sensitivity will be a by-product of learning to resist the busyness of our culture. Busy people are simply too busy to see the opportunities around them; they are too busy to hear God urging them to talk to this person or that. Conversely those of us who have time are generally more willing to be generous with it.

WHERE ARE THE PUBLIC SQUARES?

Overcoming the taboos with which our society surrounds the stranger is hard enough. Trying to participate freely in public life is still more difficult.

It is particularly difficult for Christians because of the privatization of which we have spoken. The modern world assumes that religion is a private affair. Thus, when Christians attempt to express a specifically Christian perspective on some public issue, they are likely to be told that they should not meddle in politics. But, if we acquiesce, 'the public arena is left to its own unchallenged devices while God is known at the edges by adherents who sustain themselves spiritually and offer to ameliorate pastorally the worst sufferings of the world's victims'.[9]

A more general reason is the high degree of institutionalization which has overtaken public life in the West. The individual who wants to be involved in local or national politics rapidly finds that there are no open spaces. Every space is filled with structures of one sort or another. Thus political involvement comes to mean membership of a political party, a trade union or some other pressure group.

One of the 'successes' of modernity has been this creation of the illusion of democracy while withholding the substance. For most people, engagement in public life is limited to the few minutes required every four years or so to attend the local polling station and put a cross on a piece of paper. In contrast, genuine democracy would be incredibly time-intensive. We once visited a part of the United States where local government is still conducted by means of the town meeting. What this means is a commitment on the part of every member of the community to give up several evenings a year to meet for major policy decisions (and, from time to time, to elect an executive to act on their behalf). On such evenings the hall of the local high school is crammed with several thousand people!

Where can people find the time for informal free discussion? The example of the churches in Eastern Europe (particularly what was formerly East Germany) suggests that we possess an unrecognized resource. In a totalitarian situation it was the churches which provided the space and time in which people could voice their concerns and dissent.

Perhaps one way in which we could contribute to the regeneration of political life is by encouraging our churches to offer such spaces (times) to people in our own society. This does not mean meetings in which some expert gives 'the Christian perspective' on an issue and then fields questions. Rather it means hospitality writ large: offering the strangers who share our public world the security of time and space on church premises so that they may share their concerns with us and with one another. Thus the church has the potential to become 'a community which frees us from the insularity of private life and leads to a creative public life'.[10]

TIME FOR CREATION

> Six hours in sleep, in law's grave study six,
> Four spend in prayer, the rest on nature fix.
> (Sir Edward Coke)

According to this reckoning, a good jurist of the sixteenth century could expect to spend eight hours a day enjoying God's good creation! While proportions may have changed according to circumstances and 'enjoyment' might not be the most appropriate term to use, it is certainly true that for most of human history the majority of human beings have lived close to nature.

It was only with the advent of urbanization and our time-hungry society that this began to change to any significant degree. Today hundreds of millions of men, women and children around the globe live lives more or less alienated from the natural world which is our most fundamental physical environment.

In contrast to the largely artificial lives of present-day city dwellers, human beings were created to have an intimate relationship with their natural environment. Genesis envisages men and women as the curators of God's good creation; our purpose in relation to the earth – 'to work it and take care of it' (Gen. 2:15). Arguably a rounded view of human health (such as is suggested by the biblical concept of *shalom*) will include a healthy interaction with the natural environment. Edith Schaeffer, for one, suggests that

> Man does not have the same healthy refreshment for his nervous or his physical system if he never gets his feet on the earth, and his eyes, nostrils, ears, and taste buds free from the sights, sounds, flavours and smells of machine, concrete, exhaust and other non-natural things.[11]

Again it is no easy thing to find time for the enjoyment of God's good creation. So many man-made attractions vie for our attention that nature is easily marginalized. Instead of the reality perhaps we settle for carefully packaged images on some television programme – a merely vicarious experience of the natural world. Two decades ago Edith Schaeffer could say that, 'It takes will power and determination in today's world to take a day off to walk or hike, to become tired yet refreshed through physical effort in the setting of the beauty and quietness of nature'.[12] It has not become any easier in the intervening years. At the same time the urgency of taking time to enjoy God's good creation has increased sharply.

5. Exercises

a. Time for nature

When was the last time you spent some time walking in your local park or in the countryside? Last week? Last month? Why not set aside some time this week to get back in touch with the natural world in some way.

b. The road to involvement

The theologian Karl Barth advised people to pray with a Bible in one hand and a newspaper in the other. This has a twofold effect. It is a way of bringing matters of public concern before God. But, as we pray over the news, it also tends to make us particularly conscious of certain events or situations. If you like, it is a way of allowing God to indicate to us matters about which we should be particularly concerned. Such continuing concern, expressed through prayer, is an essential mode of Christian involvement in the world. And, of course, it may lead to other forms of involvement such as hospitality.

c. The Lord loves justice

Social and political activists face a continual struggle against bitterness and judgmentalism. It is hard to maintain hope when the entire system seems to be unjust. But Psalm 33 offers us a different perspective. Try reading it prayerfully several times. Read it in the light of the historical reality of ancient Israel: an insignificant state founded by runaway slaves which was dominated by one foreign power after another. What then was the basis for the psalmist's joy? What was the basis of his hope?

7

Time for Work

I once worked simultaneously for two large church boards, half time in each. one was a staff of all women, the other was an executive staff dominated by men. The two staffs had very different work styles. The women had two casual prayer and sharing times a week, with doughnuts and coffee. The men had a prepared devotional by one of the ministers each Friday, but staff members were often too busy to attend. The women took a daily coffee break where executives and clerical staff all caught up on each other's lives. The men drank coffee at their desks. The women met once a month for a potluck lunch to hear about staff conferences and to celebrate joys like the birth of a great-niece. The men met once a week for a bag-lunch staff meeting. The women had a monthly birthday party. The men never had a party except for evening (after-hours) dinners. The women expected staff members who traveled to take 'comp' time when they had been been on the road overnight and on weekends. The men expected staff members who traveled to be back on time the next day. Both groups accomplished enormous amounts of work. One group also had fun and made lifetime friends.[1]

THE HEART OF MODERN TIME PRESSURES

a. Where we feel the pinch

For most of us work (or lack of it) is the dominant aspect of everyday life and, hence, of our time. Modern life may be divided into public and private spheres. We are often told that the private life of a public figure has no bearing on his or her office. But it does not work the other way: the public sphere of work clearly takes priority over the private. If the job demands sacrifices, it is usually the 'private life' that is first on the altar.

The implication of this order of priorities is that all time is potentially work time. Work is the primary reality and leisure is understood as the absence of work. This is, of course, one reason why those with paid employment often believe that the unemployed have a leisurely existence! It also results in a utilitarian understanding of leisure: rest and recreation have to achieve something 'worthwhile'. Think of the extent to which advertisers stress the 'educational value' of children's toys. Consider also the proliferation of mindless toys for busy executives under the guise of aids to stress reduction: play is only acceptable if it is useful.

The belief that all time is potential work time has equally disturbing implications for work time itself. One is that work increasingly encroaches upon leisure. Far from the leisure society predicted a couple of decades ago, we are seeing the emergence of a society characterized by overwork and workaholism. People borrow more and more time from their private lives in order to satisfy their work habit. Increasingly we are becoming a society of time debtors as much as of financial debtors. As one American businessman put it, 'Busy families like mine, where we both work, sub-contract our lives'.[2]

b. The elevation of work

Why has work come to have this central place?

One simple answer to this question is to blame it on the

Protestant work ethic. The Reformers and their successors certainly placed a high value upon work. They were motivated by a desire to overcome the sacred-secular divide which restricted God to holy days and holy people. They saw *all* of life, including work, as holy. Thus secular work was, in itself, potentially a spiritual activity. However, they would have been firmly opposed to our obsession with work. They would have insisted that God should be central to our lives and would, therefore, have recognized modern busyness and workaholism as forms of idolatry.

Simple answers may be attractive but they are often misleading. The story of the elevation of work to its present central place in our lives is necessarily complex. However, two factors may be highlighted as particularly significant in this regard.

One factor is the centrality of the market economy in modern life. Arguably it has taken on an almost religious aspect with journalists using the language of religious apocalyptic to describe market fluctuations. Economic concepts have penetrated into every aspect of our lives including our understanding of personal relationships (which have become 'transactions' in which we 'invest' time). The perceived omnipotence of the market was highlighted in the famous line, 'You can't buck the market.' It is not hard for the Christian to make the connection with Mammon: for many of our contemporaries the market is their object of worship. Seen in this light, the modern obsession with work may be interpreted as the sacrifice of our labour to the god of the market in the hope that it will bless us with success.

That word 'success' links to the second factor in our obsession with work. During the eighteenth and nineteenth centuries there was a steady drift away from Christian belief towards secularism. One of the first aspects of Christian belief to be affected was Christian faith in divine providence. In place of trust in the fatherly care of God, the European Enlightenment of the eighteenth century gave us an impersonal principle of harmony and the myth of progress. The principle of harmony is the 'hidden hand' which, according to secular economists, ensures that selfish behaviour is ironed out by market forces so that the market produces what is best for society as a whole (again notice the shift from trust in God to trust in the market). Thus internal forces ensure an inexorable progress towards the perfect society.

But how do we measure progress? The crudest (and most popular) measure is in terms of material success. Thus the (religious) myth of progress is given plausibility by economic growth. On a public level this results in an obsession with ever-increasing gross national products. On an individual level it leads to an acquisitive life-style. But growth is driven by work – in order to satisfy our addiction to growth and material success we must work harder and harder.

This attitude has also led to a significant narrowing of our understanding of work. 'Real' work earns real money: workers in lowly paid jobs, part-time workers and people engaged in full-time housework are by this definition relegated to second-class status.

PUTTING WORK IN ITS PLACE

a. Work in relation to the rest of life

The institution of the Sabbath (e.g., Exod. 20:8) makes it clear that, for the biblical authors, life was to consist of both work and rest. However, the Bible does not dictate any particular model for the relationship between them. Different approaches are equally legitimate and will have their own peculiar advantages and dangers.

Some people do not distinguish between work and leisure. Their work gives them great pleasure and satisfaction. For example, we know an Anglo-Catholic priest for whom the priesthood is about the whole of life: taking his washing to the launderette or having a pint with a few friends at his local pub are as much priestly acts as celebrating the Eucharist. He rarely takes holidays but, on the other hand, the whole of his life is permeated by a leisureliness which is rare in our busy age. The peculiar dangers of such an approach to work and leisure are, of course, idleness and workaholism. If work and leisure are confused we may pretend that we are working when in fact we are not (e.g., some of the clergymen in the novels of Jane Austen or Trollope). Conversely, and more probably under modern conditions, work will expand to fill every waking moment.

Alternatively work and leisure may be seen in polar relationship. Thus leisure may be regarded as having a compensatory role – during leisure we exercise and develop those faculties and aspects of our personality which are left untouched by our work. Thus the sedentary office worker may choose active leisure pursuits; someone who spends a lot of time relating to other people may feel the need for solitude; someone whose work demands considerable mental activity may seek contemplative or manual leisure activities. There is much to commend such an approach. The danger, of course, is that, given our obsession with work, leisure easily comes to be seen as subordinate – it is not an equally important part of life but merely a way of refreshing us so that we can go on working.

Yet another possibility is to regard work and leisure as entirely autonomous, as separate compartments into which the week is divided. Again the danger of this approach is that 'real life' will be identified with one part of the rhythm – usually the work part.

Biblical teaching on work and leisure is flexible enough to accommodate any of these models. The Bible sees both work and leisure as good. What it rejects is any attempt to turn either into an absolute good. Idleness is explicitly condemned (2 Thess. 3:10f) while workaholism is undermined by the injunction to rest.

b. Work and the Sabbath

For Christians, neither work nor leisure should be the central reality of our lives. That place is reserved exclusively for God. Sabbath rest is a potent symbol of the revolution implicit in making God rather than work the centre of life. Its importance was not lost on Voltaire. He once commented that 'If you wish to destroy the Christian religion you must first destroy the Christian Sunday.'

The Sabbath has several purposes in biblical thought. Particularly relevant at this point is that it puts work (and activity in general) in its proper perspective. It is a symbolic reminder that there is more to life than work, that work was made for humankind not humankind for work. If our daily work is an expression of our God-given dominion over creation, Sabbath rest is an expression of our dominion over the world of work. That tireless social reformer William Wilberforce recognized its importance when he said, 'Blessed be to God for the day of rest and religious occupation wherein earthly things assume their true size. Ambition is stunted.'

Sabbath rest rescues work from becoming an end in itself. It gives us an opportunity to recall the God-given purposes of work. Thus it restores the meaning to our work. It follows that, in the present climate of obsession with work, Christians should be in the forefront of those pressing for the preservation of genuine rest and leisure periods.

However, if we are to be taken seriously, we must begin by putting our own house in order. How many Christians campaign vigorously for shops to remain shut on Sunday, but then spend Sundays trying to maintain a frenetic schedule of religious work? How many of us find it only too easy to identify with the American clergyman who said, 'I'm sure glad that there is only one rest day per week, I'd burn out if we had to go through two "days of rest" like this every seven days'![3] If we find that Sunday is too full of religious activities to be our Sabbath, then we must find another regular day to become our day of rest.

c. Subversive Christianity

The Nobel prize-winning economist Milton Friedman once commented that 'Few trends could so thoroughly undermine the very foundations of our free society as the acceptance by corporate officials of a social responsibility other than to make as much money for their stockholders as possible. This is a fundamentally subversive doctrine.'[4] By his standards, Christianity, with its insistence that there is more to life than making money, is a subversive doctrine! Taking a stand against the individual and corporate workaholism that we encounter implies that we will be taking a stand against the central values of contemporary culture.

Such a stand is likely to be costly. On a personal level it will entail ridicule and contempt (terms like 'clock-watcher' and 'shirker' are regularly applied to those who refuse to make their work the be-all and end-all). On a corporate level, refusal to overwork may damage your prospects of promotion and, in the present economic climate, may jeopardize your job.

WORK AS VOCATION

Work may not be the most important thing in life but it is, nevertheless, good. One way Christianity has underlined this had been to describe work as a vocation.

a. The call of God

First and foremost God calls us to enter into a personal relationship with him. This is already implicit in Genesis 1 when human beings are made in the image of God. In the light of the Christian belief that God is fundamentally a unity of three persons, being God's image means being persons-in-relationship. Christ's reconciling activity enables us once more to enter into a proper personal relationship with God, with each other and with the natural world.

However, vocation is often used in a secondary sense to describe God's call to specific tasks through which we give practical expression to our renewed relationships. When we describe work as a vocation, we are using the term in this secondary sense.

b. Finding the right job

Today we often speak about 'feeling called'. To do so stresses the subjective dimension of vocation. However, biblical realism also demands that we take into account the objective dimension.

This may be seen in the fact that the Bible *assumes* that calling begins where you are. The disciples were explicitly called to follow Jesus. By contrast, Jesus' response to the man who was Legion makes it clear that his calling was to return home. The same is true of the Samaritan woman in John 4. Paul generalizes this in his correspondence with the Corinthians: 'in whatever state each was called, there let him remain with God' (1 Cor. 7:24 RSV).

If you are still uneasy about whether your present situation is God's vocation, the God-given purposes of work offer objective criteria. If your job is moral; if it provides you with an opportunity to serve others (directly or indirectly); if it is personally fulfilling; and, if you can offer it to God as an act of worship, then there is every reason to believe that this is where you should remain. Furthermore, if you are seeing positive results in your work, these may be taken as confirmation that this is God's call.

If you still believe that God may be calling you to some other sphere of activity, those same criteria may be used to assess the various alternatives which present themselves to you.

Two other comments are worth making about seeking God's will. One is that, generally speaking, God does not have a single ideal blueprint for your life which you may thwart by an incorrect decision. Too many Christians are burdened by an entirely unnecessary sense that they have missed God's perfect will for their lives. Such a view is, in fact, a denial of God's sovereignty. Nothing we do can thwart God's will; we may find that he takes us by a roundabout path to get there; but God is interested in the ultimate end rather than in the details of the various paths by which we might reach it.

The other point to make, specifically in connection with work, is that biblical teaching does not permit us to set up a hierarchy of jobs. It is not more spiritual to be a pastor or a missionary than to be a street cleaner. As Luther once pointed out, 'God does not look at the insignificance of the acts but at the heart that serves Him in such little things.'

c. The implications for our work

Seeing our work (whether paid or unpaid) as God's calling invests it with spiritual significance. Work is not just a way of earning money. Rather, if God has called us to do it, it is a positive part of our relationship with him. Thus, seeing our work as a divine vocation enables us to offer that work back to him as an act of worship. Dorothy Sayers saw this more clearly than most when she wrote,

> It is not right to acquiesce in the notion that a man's life is divided into the time he spends on his work and the time he spends in serving God. He must be able to serve God in his work, and the work itself must be accepted and respected as the medium of divine creation.[5]

Such an outlook restores the dignity to menial tasks. It also protects work from the pressure to make the product the be-all and end-all by restoring the service of God and humankind as the true goal of human work.

Secondly, seeing work as vocation means that this is where God wants us to be. Without this perspective, our only criteria for judging work are material success and personal fulfilment. As a result, we are always on the look out for some other form of work which might be more rewarding financially and/or personally. Thus it overcomes the 'grass is greener' syndrome: it enables us to be contented in our work.

Finally, seeing this sphere of work as God's calling enables us to approach it wholeheartedly.

If we are content in our work, see it as an offering to God and approach it wholeheartedly we are well protected against other people's priorities. Commenting on the importance of hearing God's call, Robert Banks suggests that 'We will gain more time by properly understanding his will for us than by all the time-saving suggestions put together'.[6] In other words, seeing our work as a vocation should enable us to give it boundaries: if God has called me to do this, I will devote myself to this rather than that.

MANAGING WORK TIME

Work is the sphere of life in which time management really comes into its own and much of the advice which follows is gleaned ultimately from that sphere. However, we are assuming a Christian perspective on all of these activities. In other words, we assume that Christians who wish to use these ideas will do their planning in a context of prayer. For example, as you assign priorities to the tasks that confront you, you should do so prayerfully, open to the real possibility that God will nudge you to alter your priorities.

a. Cutting through the undergrowth

Modern life is an uncharted jungle of possibilities and demands. Clarity of vision is absolutely essential if we are to handle such complexity in a responsible manner.

(i) Vision
Thus the prerequisite for a Christian approach to time management is hearing God's call. If you know that God wants you

here rather than there, it immediately gives you a firm vantage point from which to observe the jungle around you.

But God's call is never just static. If God has called you to be here, it is not merely to maintain the status quo. On the contrary, Christian vocations are better understood in terms of pilgrimage. God calls us to follow him and this job or that job is the means.

Thus along with the vocation God will give the vision. Without a vision the people perish, the Bible tells us. Why? Because God's pilgrim people need to know their path through the wilderness. Without a vision, the way is unclear. Returning to the jungle metaphor, vision enables us to cut through the undergrowth. All the time-saving exercises in the world will be of no use to you without a vision. There is a passage in *Alice in Wonderland* which expresses our need for a sense of direction. Alice asks the Cheshire Cat which way she should go:

> 'That depends a good deal on where you want to get to,' said the cat.
>
> 'I don't much care where . . .' said Alice.
>
> 'Then it doesn't matter which way you go,' replied the Cat.

A life vision is not something that emerges instantly without a process of reflection and refinement. An exercise which may be of some help in this process is included at the end of the chapter.

(ii) Goals

Once you know the overall direction which you want to take, the next step is to define a number of goals which will help to take you in that direction (see exercise (b) at the end of the chapter).

The essence of a goal is that it should be visibly achievable. In July 1952 Florence Chadwick set out to be the first woman to swim from Catalina to mainland California. The water was icy and the fog was thick. Her escorts had to scare off sharks on several occasions. More than fifteen hours later she gave up.

Her trainer told her she was nearly there and urged her on, but all she could see was the fog. She was pulled out only half a mile short of her goal. When asked later why she had failed, she replied, 'If I could have seen the land, I could have made it. When you're out there swimming and you can't see your goal, you lose all sense of progress and you begin to give up.' Two months later she tried again and beat the men's record by two hours.

A goal may have to be broken down into sub-goals in order to make it achievable. This is a common practice amongst mountaineers: a climb may be divided up into stages or pitches. Nehemiah clearly knew how to set realistic goals. Rebuilding the walls of Jerusalem was a major task but in Nehemiah 3 we find that manageable portions of the wall were assigned to each task force.

(iii) Priorities

Having defined your goals, the time has come to set your priorities. Some goals may be more important and/or urgent than others. Efficient use of your time depends on knowing which goals should take priority. For example, the completion of this book is less urgent but more important than a book review Lawrence has agreed to do. Given that the deadline for the review is approaching it is tempting to complete that first. However a delay in completing this chapter is likely to have a knock-on effect on the rest of the book. Therefore this chapter takes priority over the book review which, in turn, takes priority over other items on our list.

One simple way of assigning priorities to a list of 'things to do' is to consider each item in turn: if it must be done today (or, perhaps, this week or this month) mark it with an A; if it would be good but not essential to complete it within the time-scale under consideration, mark it with a B; if it can wait, mark it with a C.

Having gone through the entire list, reconsider the items marked with an A. Do you have too many items for this period of time? If so, go through your 'A' priorities, grading them 1, 2 and 3 according to their importance. If you find it impossible to decide between any two items, choose on the basis of their urgency.

When deciding longer-term priorities, it is helpful to think about where your strengths and weaknesses really lie. It has been suggested that perhaps 80 per cent of our output comes from about 20 per cent of our time. In other words, routine matters, time wasters and time invested in areas of weakness may account for up to 80 per cent of our working time. As we look at the tasks which lie ahead, it is helpful to try and maximize the time which will be spent on genuinely productive tasks.

Of course, productivity may be defined in different ways. For example, Diana's area of strength is pastoral care. Therefore in planning the best use of their time, the parish leadership team might steer pastoral problems in her direction while pushing more of the parish administration in the direction of another leader who is a gifted administrator. Another potential application of the 80–20 rule is to housework: we have heard it said that 80 per cent of the dirt and untidiness accumulates in 20 per cent of the house. Thus you can save a good deal of time on housework by identifying that 20 per cent and concentrating your cleaning efforts in it, leaving the other 80 per cent of the house until it really needs cleaning!

b. Finding the time

But having a sense of direction and planning the way forward is only half the battle in the world of time management. Equally important is finding the time to put your plans into practice. This consists of three main elements: knowing your current use of time; identifying and reducing those factors which waste your time; and, re-scheduling the time won back from time wasters so that it can be put to constructive use. As Gordon Macdonald points out, 'If my private world is in order, it is because I have begun to seal the "time leaks" and allocate my productive hours in the light of my capabilities, my limits, and my priorities'.[7]

(i) Consolidation

Knowing how we use our time and tackling time wasters have already been dealt with in Chapter 3. But gaining time in this way is not enough. There is little point in paring a couple of minutes off the average length of your telephone calls unless you can somehow consolidate those minutes into useable blocks of time. This brings up the whole field of detailed time planning, of keeping a diary. Detailed day to day planning allows you to make more efficient use of your time. For example, blocking all your phone calls together is a more efficient way of handling the telephone than scattering them throughout the day. As with other aspects of time management, entire books are available on how to plan your time from day to day to achieve maximum efficiency.[8]

(ii) Delegation

Time for the really important tasks can be maximized by delegating wherever possible. Moses was fortunate enough to have a father-in-law who understood the wisdom of delegation. In Exodus 18:13 we find Moses attempting singlehandedly to settle everyone's problems. Jethro's advice is unequivocal: 'What you are doing is not good. You and these people who come to you will only wear yourselves out' (Exod. 18:17f). He goes on to tell Moses to delegate the simpler cases to reliable men. Sir Fred Catherwood recommends that 'The only jobs we should aim to keep are those that no one else in sight is capable of doing'.[9]

Of course delegation is not always about time saving. Very often we must delegate in order to encourage the personal development of colleagues. One of the reasons for Napoleon's success was his practice of delegating to his senior commanders – giving them responsibility made his army much more efficient than if they had to refer everything back to him. In the home we delegate certain tasks to the children: they are responsible for preparing their own packed lunches, they are expected to keep their rooms tidy and put away their toys. This takes longer and the results are often less than perfect. But they are growing in personal responsibility.

(iii) Using scraps of time

A piano teacher once warned his pupil not to practise in long stretches: 'When you grow up, time won't come in long stretches. Practise in minutes, whenever you can find them ... and music will become a part of your life.' That child grew up to become a successful author by writing a hundred words or so whenever he had a few minutes to spare. John le Carré wrote *The Spy Who Came in From the Cold* while commuting to work. Lawrence learnt Greek by carrying flash cards with him and glancing at them in odd moments.

All of us spend some time waiting to catch trains, or queuing in banks or supermarkets. In fact, someone once estimated that we spend about a year of our lives just waiting! That time can be used for reading, writing, learning a language, praying.

c. A means not an end

Finally, never forget that time management is only a means to an end. When it becomes an end in itself, we are in real danger of turning it into an idol. By all means use time management principles to make your working practices more efficient but beware of allowing them to make you less human or of imposing their dehumanizing possibilities on your subordinates. As a warning of the dangers of an insensitive use of time management, consider the following statement by a former airline reservations clerk:

> You were allowed no more than three minutes on the telephone. You had twenty seconds, 'busy-out' time it was called, to put the information in. Then you had to be available for another phone call. It was almost like a production line. We adjusted to the machine. The casualness, the informality that

had been there previously were no longer there. They monitored you and listened to your conversations. If you were a minute late for work it went on your file. You took thirty minutes for lunch, not thirty-one! If you got a break you took ten minutes, not eleven! I was on eight tranquillisers a day. With the airline I had no free will. I was just part of the stupid computer.[10]

The moral of the story is, 'Don't put minutes before people'!

5. Exercises

a. Building your vision

Visions begin with dreams. What is your dream for your life? Spend a few minutes prayerfully reflecting on this question. Ask God to help you put into words what 'fulfilment' would mean in your life. When you are ready, write out your life dream.

How does a dream become a vision, a genuine motivating factor for your life? One Christian management consultant suggests four criteria: it must be clear; it must make a distinct impression on people; it must be lasting (i.e., something that you have lived with for some time or has captured your imagination); and it must require you to change (since Christians are a pilgrim people, an authentic Christian vision is unlikely merely to endorse the status quo). Check your dream against these criteria. Can you sharpen up your dream statement in any way?

Finally, share your vision with someone else. Talking it over will help you clarify it further. Making it public will strengthen your commitment to that vision.

b. From vision to goals

If a life vision may be likened to our ultimate destination, goals are landmarks on the way. They are achievable targets.

The first step in the transition from vision to goals is to ask yourself, 'How will I know that I am making progress towards my vision?' Reflect on this and write down four or five answers.

Peter Brierley suggests that goals should be **SMART:** Specific, Measurable, Achievable, Realistic and Timed.

Take one of your answers and revise it until it meets these criteria. For example, if one of your answers was, 'I would be spending more time with my spouse', the corresponding goal might be 'to arrange my schedule so that within three months I am spending every Friday night with him/her.'

c. Plans for prosperity

Read Jeremiah 29:11–13. Consider your plans in the light of this passage. God has plans too – plans, without which your plans would come to nothing. What implications does this truth have for your plans?

8

Time for the Church

Once upon a time there was a dangerous seacoast where many ships were wrecked. Volunteers from a nearby village would risk their lives to rescue sailors from drowning. Those who were saved often joined the rescue corps.

One day a volunteer suggested that they should practice. So that is what they did and were later able to save more lives. Someone else suggested building a boat house near the coast to save time. Later they added a shelter for the people they rescued, who often died of the cold, and a kitchen to make soup to warm the victims. All this made them more effective.

Later someone suggested that they wait in the boat house during storms to be ready in case of shipwreck. Another proposed adding a games room to prevent boredom, a third that they expand the kitchen. This grew into a member's lounge and restaurant. The rescue station grew in prestige, and many more joined it for this reason.

As time passed someone pointed out that rescuing was a skilled task demanding specialized training. So they hired young men to do the job while the rest cheered them on from the rescue complex. Finally the members decided to abandon lifesaving; it was too costly, and they were too busy with 'club' committee meetings.

A number resigned in protest and started a real lifesaving station down the coast. Once more they braved the storms to rescue the drowning. After a while, one of their number suggested that they practice to improve their lifesaving skills. Later someone suggested that they build a boat house. Then they added a shelter and a kitchen. Eventually, they too came to regard rescuing as a specialist skill. And finally they abandoned it as too costly and too time-consuming.

A number resigned in protest.... It is said that if we visit that coast today, we will find a series of exclusive clubs, up and down the coast. None of them is interested in lifesaving, although ships are still wrecked and many people drown.[1]

INTRODUCTION

The New Testament offers a rich variety of metaphors for the entity we know as the church. Perhaps the most striking is that of the church as a body: the body of Christ (1 Cor. 12:27, Eph. 4:12, 5:23) and Christians are interdependent just like the organs of a body (1 Cor. 12:12–26). Another common Pauline metaphor is that of the family or household: the church is the family of believers (Gal. 6:10) and the household of God (Eph. 2:19, 1 Tim 3:15). And this image of the church as a family has clear resonances with Jesus' own description of his relationship with the disciples (e.g., Matt. 10:25). Elsewhere Paul describes the church in more literal terms as a fellowship (1 Cor. 5:2) and uses the term dynamically to describe our relationship with each other (Gal. 2:9) and with Christ (1 Cor. 1:9). To this brief summary it is certainly worth adding some famous words from a non-Pauline source: 'you are a chosen people, a royal priesthood, a holy nation, a people belonging to God' (1 Pet. 2:9).

The dominant theme in these images is *relationship*. Even the image of the Church as a nation implies an organic relationship with the head of state since it assumes the Old Testament's understanding of kingship and authority. Membership of the Church implies recognition of the fact of one's interdependence with *all* who claim allegiance to Christ. We are all part of God's family: an inclusive extended family which, ultimately, resists being privatized. So the New Testament view of the Church is primarily to do with personal relationships – relationships which are being transformed by our primary personal relationship with God.

In keeping with that emphasis, the characteristic actions of the church in the New Testament are: caring for one another, eating together and worshipping together. Thus the church is not seen as one activity competing with many others for the time and attention of Christians. On the contrary, it is the reworked web of personal relationships which forms the context for the Christian's everyday life.

This understanding of the church stands in sharp contrast to the experience of many contemporary Christians. The phenomenon of the church widow or widower (the person whose spouse is so enmeshed in the life of the local church that he or she seems to be out every night of the week) is only too familiar. Think of all the meetings which spring up around a church. Quite apart from Sunday worship itself there are midweek services, housegroups, Bible studies, prayer meetings, Sunday schools, youth organizations. Then there are all the meetings needed to keep those meetings going: the sidesmen's meetings, choir practices, Sunday school teachers' meetings, PCC meetings, elders' meetings, housegroup leaders' meetings, building committees, standing committees. And as if this were not enough we can fill our evenings and weekends with training courses on everything from evangelism to time management for Christians!

Significant portions of the contemporary Church seem to be bent on creating hyper-active Christians. Some Christian leaders even seem to see this hyper-activity as a sign of success. The reaction of one such person to some of the ideas in this book was, 'We don't want people to feel guilty about doing too much. They might start giving up things in order to pray'!

For too many Christians today the church has become just one more leisure activity (possibly their most demanding leisure activity): a black hole absorbing their time, energy and money, often with no visible results. As Os Guinness noted in connection with such developments in the United States: 'every meeting added, every penny collected, means less time and fewer resources for penetrating the public world'.[2]

TIME AND THE INSTITUTION

a. *The importance of structures*

Some utopian Christians believe that institutions are inimical to the Christian life – that the fellowships founded by Paul and the other apostles were completely unstructured. But a little thought will demonstrate how naive such a view is. The very metaphors used by Paul imply structure: a family, if it is to be anything more than a collection of isolated individuals living under one roof, must have a structure; a body is a highly structured entity – indeed loss of structure (or decomposition) is a sure sign that the body is dead! If the Church is to be a social reality it must have institutional structures.

If you like, the institutions of the Church are the bones of the body of Christ. They play a vital role in providing us with the framework within which we can begin to establish the relationships which constitute the living Church. As such they are worthy of our respect. However, it is worth adding that, if the body is healthy, the bones will not be too prominent!

b. *Where do we find our structures?*

Surprisingly the New Testament has little to say about church structures in spite of the fact that it presents the Church as an integral part of Christ's continuing mission to the world. Various ministries and leadership roles are mentioned but they are never clearly defined and the lists even appear to conflict with one another. One is left with the impression that much remained unspoken precisely to encourage flexibility.

Paul's ideal was to be a Jew to Jews and a Gentile to Gentiles

(1 Cor. 9:20–3). But 'Jew' and 'Gentile' are terms which imply a relationship to a community. In order to be a Jew to Jews, Paul would have had to participate in the Jewish community and its social structures. This is a fundamental of effective Christian missions. For example, Hudson Taylor made an unprecedented impact upon nineteenth-century China because he abandoned the protection of western structures and customs in favour of Chinese dress, habits and company. Similarly a mission oriented church will (as far as possible) adapt to the social structures of the people to whom it has been sent.

This process of change and adaptation is right and proper. A missionary church must adapt to its culture. Of course new structures must always be questioned in the light of the gospel. Is this an appropriate vehicle for expressing the gospel? Does it strengthen personal relationships and empower Christians for service? Or does it dehumanize and disempower?

What has this to do with our attitude to and use of time? The answer lies in the fact that fundamental ideas, attitudes and assumptions do not belong merely to some rarefied intellectual dimension. On the contrary they will be embodied in social structures. Thus a culture's attitude to time will be reflected in its customs, its laws and its social institutions. Societies which place little importance upon clock time do not, as a rule, go to great trouble to put clocks in prominent places. Nor do they present people with gold watches upon retirement!

By adopting a particular social structure or institution, the Church will inevitably appear to give approval to the assumptions built into that structure. Thus the adaptation of the early church to the culture of Imperial Rome resulted in the adoption of a hierarchical view of ministry which exists to this day in many of the older churches.

c. Modernity and the Church of God plc

Adapting to the modern world implies the adoption of modern institutional structures by the Church. This has been particularly noticeable in some of the newer American churches as well as in para-church organizations such as the World Council of Churches. Increasingly churches and related organizations are modelling themselves upon secular corporate structures. Thus we find a greater emphasis on bureaucracy and management by committee. Clergy in-service training often features courses on management techniques (including time management). We even have the Christian equivalent of a trade fair: the Christian Resources Exhibition.

Nor are utopian Christians an exception to this tendency to adapt to the culture. Far from rejecting institutional structures, they look to the counter culture for their institutions. Thus communities and networks are 'in' for radical Christians. Good examples would be the Sojourners Community and, to a lesser extent, the Iona Community.

Such adaptation is quite proper. It is part of the mission of the Church to identify with the communities to which it has been sent. Thus the adoption of modern structures and the application of modern insights from such areas as sociology (e.g. in the church growth movement), business management (e.g., many courses in Christian leadership) and psycho-analysis (e.g., some of the newer approaches to pastoral counselling and spiritual direction) is quite legitimate. However, the responsible application of such insights requires a careful analysis of the assumptions on which they are based. Some of those assumptions will be carried into question by the gospel.

Unfortunately such analysis is not always evident, particularly in relation to the underlying attitudes to time. As a result efforts to adapt secular corporate structures to church life have been a window through which the dominant western view of time has been able to penetrate the church. The emergence of 'the Church plc' has been accompanied by an increasing acceptance of secular attitudes to time.

Hyper-active churches display an obsession with church activities which parallels the contemporary obsession with work described in Chapter 7. Their leaders are under pressure for the church to be 'successful'. But how do you measure 'success' in church life? The answer is usually by looking for some kind of growth: growth in numbers of members is the simplest yardstick; it may be growth in the numbers seeking counselling, spiritual direction or making confessions; growth in particular activities (membership of housegroups, youth work, etc) is another yardstick; perhaps the crudest measure (but one that is only too evident in some churches) is growth in financial commitment to the church and growth in capital expenditure. Closely related to an obsession with growth is a proliferation of programmes: techniques to help us become more successful as a church.

We know of one hyper-active church where the minister has set himself a target of one hundred pastoral visits per month! Such an attitude easily spills over into the congregation as a whole until much of the active membership is over-committed to church activities. By setting an unrealistic example, ministers may inadvertently build a kind of guilt complex into their congregation. Thus on advising an overworked churchwarden to take things easy you may get the response, 'But the vicar works so hard, this is the least I can do!'

Programmes are not wrong in themselves. On the contrary, they may bring new life to a dead church. But they become dangerous when they begin to take priority over people. For example, the level of visits mentioned in the previous paragraph carries with it the risk of working mechanically through the electoral roll regardless of the needs or desires of the people visited. Similarly the curate who allowed no more than fifteen minutes to a hospital visit was letting his timetable take priority over people. A visit motivated by the need to tick your name off a list has quite a different feel from a visit motivated by genuine concern! Ultimately the effect of such programmes is dehumanizing.

THERAPY FOR BUSY CHURCHES

Warning against an uncritical adoption of secular structures, the Christian sociologist Jacques Ellul points out that

> It is not [our] primary task to think out plans, programs, methods of action and achievement. When Christians do this it is simply an imitation of the world, which is doomed to defeat. The central problem which today confronts a Christian is *not* to know how to act ... [the Church's] first objective should be the creation of a style of life.[3]

Ellul reminds us that the Church is in the business of promoting a style of life rather than a programme of action. If we find our church life becoming over-busy, it is time to question our practice in the light of the essential nature of the church.

a. Reviewing our structures

Structures are good if and only if they help the Church to be what God intends it to be. Thus we should, from time to time, stand back from our institutions and ask of them:

Do they help us to worship together or do they tend to promote individual piety and spirituality?

Do they help us to learn together (and from each other) or do they tend to stifle honest questioning?

Do they empower every member to serve Christ in some way or do they tend to concentrate power in the hands of a few (the clergy and/or a handful of keen lay people)?

Do they help us to care for each other more effectively?

Do they enable us to have fun together or do they tend to make Christianity a serious matter?

Do they assist us in making the stranger feel at home or do they tend to make us introspective and exclusive?

In short, do they build up or stifle our relationships with one another and with Christ?

b. Escaping from over-institutionalization

But what can a church do if it finds that the answers to the above questions reveal that it is over-institutionalized?

(i) Cut back the dead wood

One useful starting point might be to take a critical look at the church's structure of committees, rotas and meetings. A proliferation of meetings (particularly business meetings) may well be symptomatic of a hyper-active church.

Are any of the meetings required by law or by the constitution of the church (e.g., meetings of a parochial church council or an annual meeting of all church members)? Obviously such requirements must be respected. But are we tending to increase the frequency of such meetings? If so, perhaps it is time to cut back to the constitutional requirements.

The vast majority of church meetings will be neither statutory nor required by constitution. It is well worth asking of these meetings whether they are essential – not just useful but essential. While on the subject of usefulness, it is also worth asking the precise nature of a meeting's usefulness: we know of one clergyman who promoted committee meetings because they kept keen lay people busy and made them feel important while he quietly made all the key decisions himself!

As a rule of thumb, if the active members of the church are beginning to feel burdened by the church's programme of meetings, the church is probably holding too many meetings. The only answer is radical surgery. The Christian management consultant David Cormack recalls the following dialogue with a harassed manager:

> 'Just look at my diary!' he complained to me. 'More than three days a week in meetings! What do you suggest?'
>
> I replied, 'Begin by cancelling one meeting in three and reducing the remainder by half.' He said, 'But I don't know which ones are important.' My reply was: 'True. But your secretary will know.'

He lifted the phone and called her in. Then he said, 'Jean, I want one meeting in three cancelled – you'll know which – and every other meeting has to have its time cut by half.'

The effects of his decision were soon felt across the whole organization as other managers took his lead, meetings were cancelled, paper work was reduced and time was made available for the real work.[4]

Over the years we have been involved in a variety of churches with committee structures of widely differing sizes and degrees of complexity. One thing stands out clearly from our experience: the spiritual life of a congregation bears little relation to the complexity of its committee structure. Many churches *could* survive (and thrive) with fewer meetings. The same is also true of larger Christian organizations. For example, some years ago one Anglican diocese proved itself quite able to give up meetings for Lent!

(ii) Meet for a purpose

A second step in tackling church hyper-activity is to insist that all structures should be regarded as temporary. Church structures should only exist for a specific purpose. When that purpose is fulfilled the structure should be dissolved. Similarly when conditions have changed or people with the appropriate gifts have moved on, the structure should be dissolved. Few things are more pathetic than a church seeking to meet needs that no longer exist or struggling to maintain a programme set in place by some gifted individual who moved away years ago. Nothing is sacrosanct. The fact that twenty years ago God gifted your church with able youth workers is not sufficient reason for you to struggle to maintain a dying structure with inadequate staff. Far better to ask what God wants you to do with the gifts he has given you today. Thus *all* church structures should be subjected to regular critical review.

(iii) Small is beautiful

Another way to avoid unnecessary bureaucracy is to decentralize wherever possible. If personal relationships are central to the nature of the Church, structures which promote deeper personal relationships should be favoured. It is well known that small groups build up relationships more effectively than large meetings. Therefore the emphasis should shift from central church meetings to homegroups (housegroups, cell groups, base communities or whatever you prefer to call them).

(iv) Worship is central

Last and perhaps most important is to re-emphasize that the church is essentially a *worshipping* community. As Eastern Orthodoxy has always maintained and the charismatic movement has recently rediscovered, when we enter into worship we step out of secular time into God's time.

The Australian theologian Robert Banks makes a radical suggestion in this connection. In recognition of the fact that we are stepping out of secular time into worship, we should leave our watches outside!

Alternatively (or additionally) we may want to reschedule our service to permit a more leisurely approach to worship. For example, we might consider changing the time of the mid-morning Sunday service so that members of the congregation need not worry about Sunday lunch burning if the service goes on half an hour longer than usual.

KEEP IN STEP WITH THE SPIRIT

All the above advice could be summarized in the phrase 'Keep in step with the Spirit.' A story from Australia makes the point:

> Once upon a time there was a mighty river. It flowed gracefully and elegantly across the landscape. Along its banks it gave life and sustenance to the tribes of Aboriginal Australians who camped by it. For many generations this river was

a central focus for life. Then, gradually, the river ceased to flow, becoming a stagnant pool. With the heat of summer it started to dry up. Around the banks of the disappearing symbol of their security, the people watched aghast. What could be happening to them? By the dried-up riverbed many sat, waiting for the river to flow once more.

Yet others thought to look around and discovered that the river was not gone. Still flowing, it had simply changed course upstream, creating a billabong on the curve at which they sat.[5]

Do we prefer to sip the last drops of stagnant water from our billabong or will we venture forth in faith, trusting God to lead us to where the river of the Holy Spirit flows freely?

5. Exercises

a. Making time for mission

The writing of this book took place as many of our churches were gearing up for a Decade of Evangelism. But we believe that one of the main hindrances to evangelism is simply lack of time. Many Christians are too busy supporting church activities to build up relationships with the non-Christians around them. If you feel that this is true of you, you might like to consider giving up one church activity per week. Instead you might enrol in an evening class, join a sports club, support your local football team, visit your local pub, or anything else that brings you into contact with non-churchgoers. Choose something that you would enjoy doing and go prepared to befriend people for their own sakes.

b. Pot luck suppers

Do people in your church have little time to get to know each other? Why not organize some social events? We entitled this exercise 'pot luck suppers' because these are probably the easiest of events to organize: everyone brings something to put on the common table.

The point is to encourage table fellowship. Eating together breaks down barriers and helps to strengthen personal relationships. It also creates new possibilities for worship.

c. One body, one Spirit

Read through Eph. 4:1–16 slowly and prayerfully. This was Paul's vision for the Church. How does it relate to your experience? Does anything strike you as particularly relevant to your local church? What should you be praying for your church? What practical step can you take to bring the reality a little closer to the vision?

9

Time for God

The Curé D'Ars, an eighteenth-century French saint, once noticed that an old peasant used to sit for hours in the church: he would just sit facing the altar, apparently not even praying. At last the Curé challenged him. The peasant turned to him with a smile and said, 'I look at him, he looks at me and we are happy together.'

THE MEANING OF LIFE

What is the answer to the Question of Life, the Universe and Everything? According to *The Hitch Hiker's Guide to the Galaxy* it is 'forty-two'! For centuries Christian theologians have pondered similar questions. However, in the light of the gospel, they have arrived at a more satisfying answer. For example:

> What is the chief and highest end of man?
> Man's chief and highest end is to glorify God, and fully to enjoy him for ever.[1]

This means that time for God is the most important aspect of the Christian view of time. However what this means for our use of time is not easily comprehensible today.

Even amongst Christians who reject the privatization of religion, accommodation to secular perspectives has resulted in a compartmentalization of life. This is so pervasive that it is very difficult to speak about our use of time without using such categories. We have used these distinctions (e.g., time for work and time for leisure) for the sake of clarity. But, when they are hardened into watertight compartments, they can easily obscure the meaning of time for God.

The effect of compartmentalization is to give the impression that time for God is one of the categories into which our total time may be divided. Thus we give God so many hours per week and divide up the rest between work, self and personal relationships. Perhaps if we are particularly pious we treat our time as if it were money and give God a tithe. The net effect is to treat time for God as just one more part of our life.

On this view, time for God is a fragile commodity. One of the characteristics of modern life is competition both within and between compartments. The world of work threatens the world of leisure. Within the world of leisure there seems to be an exponential growth in choices of entertainment – all competing for our attention in a finite amount of time. It is only too easy for time for God (conventionally thought of as time for prayer, meditation, Bible study, public worship and, possibly, other Christian activities) to be squeezed out by these competing forces. Both Old and New Testaments bear witness to what might be called the self-effacing character of God: he is encountered in stillness, in the still small voice; he stands at the door and knocks and awaits our response. He does not force himself upon those who are too busy to stop and listen for that quiet knock on the door.

ALL TIME IS GOD'S TIME

This compartmentalization begins to break down when we recall that all time is God's time. But what does this mean?

God's eternal life is often contrasted with our temporal existence. Thanks largely to the influence of Hellenistic philosophy on Christian theology, this has often led Christians to suggest that eternity is the negation of time: time is associated with change and decay, eternity with changelessness and, hence, perfection. However, the result is a static God very different from the living God portrayed by the Bible. True, God is changeless but the changelessness is an expression of his faithfulness rather than a denial of his life.

A more biblical view is to see eternity as the fulfilment rather than the negation of time. From this perspective, the life of creatures in time is a pale reflection of the life of God in eternity rather than its opposite.

One of the most fundamental aspects of Christian belief is that God, specifically God the Holy Spirit, is the giver of life. God not only created but he graciously allowed creation to reflect the divine life and, ultimately, to share in that life through Jesus Christ. Since life and time are intimately related, it follows that God is also the giver of time. But the God who is faithful does not abandon his creature or his gift: if time is the gift of God then all of life is conducted under God's providential care. This, in turn, implies that meaning and hope cannot be restricted to a private sphere of life – it is not just a subjective attitude which helps us cope – but an objective reality: the hope that God promises is held out to the whole of life.

a. Meeting God in time

God encounters us personally. Personal encounters take place in time and space. Consider the encounters with God described in the Bible. Adam and Eve are encountered by God in the garden in the early evening. Again and again, God meets people at particular places and particular times.

One of the striking features of Christianity which sets it apart from many of the world's religions is the fact that it offers us a story which unfolds in time. The central clue is the story of Jesus – a Jewish carpenter turned religious teacher who lived at a historically identifiable era. Christianity claims that this story gives meaning to the entire history of creation. But this story also relates to us, giving meaning to our lives and fitting us into the larger pattern.

b. Reality as God's time

If all of time is God's gift then life cannot be compartmentalized into public and private segments (or, for that matter, into the older division between sacred and secular). God cannot be limited to our quiet times or our Sunday worship.

On the contrary, everything we do, we do with God. God is intimately present in every creaturely activity. Whether we know it or not, every action, every breath we take is permitted, enabled and directed towards fulfilment by God.

This opens up a new way of looking at every aspect of life. God is present in everything if we will but attend to him. The daily round of work and family life is every bit as sacred as Sunday worship. As George Herbert puts it:

> Teach me, my God and King,
> In all things thee to see,
> and what I do in any thing,
> To do it as for thee:
>
> All may of thee partake:
> Nothing can be so mean,
> which with this tincture, 'For Thy sake,'
> Will not grow bright and clean.
>
> A servant with this clause
> Makes drudgery divine:
> Who sweeps a room, as for thy laws,
> Makes that and the action fine.
>
> This is the famous stone
> That turneth all to gold:
> for that which God doth touch and own
> Cannot for less be told.[2]

Changing nappies, mopping floors, cleaning the toilets, even the most menial work, done for the glory of God, becomes divine service. Our motivation transforms our attitude to the activity itself.

Every part of life may be seen as part of our personal relationship with God. Our work need no longer be regarded as something which competes with our attention to God. On the contrary, God is with us in our work. As we discover the reality of this, we will find that our work actually becomes something which strengthens our personal relationship with God. Similarly God is with us in our personal relationships and leisure activities. They too can become part of that process of growing in our relationship with God. Work, leisure and relationships can all be an integral part of our spiritual disciplines.

We may find that, as we work or play, we are conscious of God's presence from time to time and can pause for a quick prayer or stop and listen to him. But personal relationships are not strengthened merely by talking to each other. One of the most powerful ways of strengthening relationships is doing things together. This is true of our relationship with God – prayer is essential but experiencing the reality of doing things together is also immensely valuable.

Herbert's philosopher's stone may also be an aid to overcoming busyness. We live in an age when it is customary to focus attention exclusively on externals: programmes, possessions, protests, experience, information. Herbert calls us back to the inner life, recollecting before any action that God is Lord of that action. The Bible calls it 'the heart'; Gordon MacDonald has described it as 'the bridge' of life and argues that it is 'the only place from which we can gain the strength to brave, or even beat, any outer turbulence'.[3]

TIMES WITH GOD

All of our time should be time for God. A woman who knew Eric Liddell, the missionary and Olympic athlete, during his years in a Japanese internment camp had this to say about the secret of his ability to handle suffering:

> Eric was a man of prayer not only at set times – though he did not like to miss a prayer meeting or communion service when such could be arranged. He talked to God, all the time, naturally, as one can who enters the 'School of Prayer' to learn this way of inner discipline. He seemed to have no weighty mental problems: his life was grounded in God, in faith, and in trust.[4]

But this should not tempt us to say that, since God is with us all the time, we don't need to schedule time specifically for God. The foundation of Eric Liddell's life of prayer was a discipline of regular prayer every morning which nothing was allowed to disturb (not even the risk of discovery by Japanese guards).

Doing things together certainly strengthens a personal relationship. But it is not enough. There also has to be communication – and not just at the superficial level that is possible while you are engaged in some activity. The kind of communication on which strong personal relationships depend is self-disclosure: opening up to another about what really matters to you, about your anxieties, about your thoughts, about your feelings for the other person.

Prayer is precisely this kind of communication. It is *not* a matter of quick fixes. Our culture is obsessed with instant achievement by means of the appropriate technique. Books claiming to tell you how to get rich quick, lose weight quick, learn a language quick, become a successful salesman/public speaker/evangelist overnight are assured of good sales. But there are no techniques for successful prayer. Prayer is not the spiritual equivalent of 'How to win friends and influence people'. It is about a personal relationship – and relationships take time. Bill Hybels rightly comments: 'Some people tell me they don't need to schedule regular time for prayer; they pray on the run. These people are kidding themselves. Just try building a marriage on the run. You can't build a relationship that way, with God or with another person.'[5]

If we accept that discipline, we are opening ourselves up to the transforming friendship with God that puts the whole of life in a new perspective. Martin Luther once commented that 'I have so much business I cannot get on without spending three hours daily in prayer.' He had discovered that, far from taking time away from other activities, regular prayer actually puts them in a new and larger context.

TIME TO SLOW DOWN

To begin with, prayer means taking time to slow down. Most of us are too busy, too active, to hear God's still small voice. Gordon MacDonald reminds us that 'Praying with a fully active mind fresh from a host of conversations and decisions is difficult, if not impossible. To pray meaningfully, the mind has to be slowed down to a reflective pace'.[6]

One approach, which has been used by Christians of all traditions for centuries, is to read a Bible passage slowly and thoughtfully. For example, you might choose a psalm or one of the many Bible-based canticles found in most prayer books: read it aloud (a most effective way of reading slowly), paying attention to each word, allowing the passage to focus your attention on God as the meaning unfolds.

Another popular technique is journalling. Many Christians have discovered the value of taking time to sit before God jotting down their impressions of what they have been doing, saying, thinking and feeling. The discipline of writing forces them to slow down and enter a more reflective state.

Relaxation and centring exercises are also effective ways

of slowing down for prayer. For example, you might sit in a comfortable position and relax your body. Then close your eyes and observe your breathing, gradually establishing a rhythm of slow, deep, even breathing. This might be accompanied by an appropriate short repetitive prayer such as the Jesus Prayer: 'Lord Jesus Christ . . . Son of the living God . . . have mercy on me . . . a sinner.' Many such exercises can be found in books about traditional Christian spirituality.

A less traditional approach might be to take a long leisurely hot bath! Many people find that a bath helps them to unwind at the end of a busy day. Why not turn your time in the tub into a time of prayer?

Yet another way of slowing down might be to sit and listen to an appropriate piece of music. Perhaps you are visually-oriented rather than musically-oriented. Is there a favourite picture which you could sit and enjoy as a preparation for prayer? Or perhaps you find that a walk in the local park is an effective way of slowing down.

We are not suggesting that you need to use any or all of these techniques. Our point is simply that, if we take our relationship with God seriously, we will want to focus our attention on him. We will not want to be distracted by the busyness of our lives. Therefore, anything which helps us to focus on God is an aid to prayer.

TIME TO SHARE

Having slowed down, in whatever way, prayer requires time in which to share our concerns. This has two aspects: there will be things which we need to confess and there will be things which we want to ask of God (either on our own behalf or for others).

Intercessory prayer is sometimes caricatured as 'shopping list' prayer. Sometimes it can degenerate into little more than a list of requests which we put before God. But perhaps this is because we are too busy to get beneath the surface. We need to take time to bring the matters which really concern us to consciousness and then to share these matters with God. At times we may be unable to articulate our most deep-seated concerns. But, if we are open to God, we may share Paul's discovery that 'the Spirit helps us in our weakness. We do not know what we ought to pray for, but the Spirit himself intercedes for us with groans that words cannot express' (Rom. 8:26).

Such prayer is about unburdening ourselves of our concerns rather than presenting God with a shopping list. And this brings us to the other aspect of taking time to share. Not only do we need to unburden ourselves of our concerns and anxieties but we need to unburden ourselves of our guilt and sin. Confession and supplication together make up one pole of the self-disclosure which is necessary for a personal relationship with God.

TIME TO LISTEN

Prayer is not a monologue. Since it is central to a personal relationship (and, furthermore, a relationship initiated by God), it also involves time to listen to God.

We listen to God, in the first place, by reading the Bible. However, there are many ways of reading the Bible. Some are more helpful than others when it comes to developing a personal relationship with God. One approach might be to treat it as a love letter from God. As we read it, expecting to hear God speaking through its words we will discover with Paul that 'All Scripture is God-breathed and is useful for teaching, rebuking, correcting and training in righteousness' (2 Tim. 3:16).

Reading the Bible is a fundamental part of what it means to listen to God. But God is not limited by the words of Scripture. He can and does speak in other ways.

If we are receptive, we may hear him challenging or comforting us through the words of a sermon.

God may speak, if we are prepared to listen, through our dreams. For that reason, many Christians find it beneficial to keep a notebook at the side of their bed in which to record their dreams.

What about nature? John Newton, Jonathan Edwards and Martin Luther all heard God speak in storms.

A news report, a few words from a friend, something we read in a book or a still small voice in moments of quietness – God can use all of these and other means to speak to us.

Thus we might like to create opportunities for God to speak in other ways (e.g., including periods of silent waiting before God in our times of prayer). In such times of quietness God may speak to us through images thrown up by our imagination or through ideas which seem to come unbidden into our heads. Less commonly we may see visions or hear an inner voice addressing us.

Of course not all our imaginings, inner voices and dreams are messages from God! The admonition to 'test the spirits to see whether they are from God' (1 John 4:1) is extremely good advice. If we would listen to God, we must learn discernment.

How do we know whether some inner leading or dream is of God? One important check is whether it is consistent with Scripture. God is not limited by Scripture and the Bible certainly does not exhaust all that God wants to say to the human race. However, God is absolutely faithful and, therefore, consistent. Thus nothing that is of God will contradict what is clearly taught in Scripture. For example, if an inner voice tells you to have an affair with someone else's husband or wife, you can be certain that voice is not of God!

Of course, many leadings will not be ruled out by Scripture. The Bible will not help if you feel you are being called to become a missionary to darkest Surbiton or Little Snoring in the Marsh. But the Christian life is not a private affair between you and God. There is an essential communal dimension: the Church. Theologians used to say that outside the Church there is no salvation, not because they thought church membership brought salvation but rather because the process of being saved brought church membership! If you are a Christian you are part of the body of Christ, the Church – whether you recognize it or not. That communal dimension is vitally important in discerning the spirits. If we believe that God is telling us to do something we have a duty to share it with others, specifically, with mature Christians whom we can trust. If it stands up to their scrutiny, it is probable that the leading is of God.

TIME TO ENJOY GOD

Metropolitan Anthony recounts the following anecdote:

> One of the first people who came to me for advice when I was ordained was an old lady who said: 'Father, I have been praying almost unceasingly for almost fourteen years, and I have never had any sense of God's presence.' So I said: 'Did you give him a chance to put in a word?' 'Oh well,' she said. 'No, I have been talking to him all the time, because is not that prayer?' I said: 'No, I do not think it is, and what I suggest is that you should set apart fifteen minutes a day, sit and just knit before the face of God.' And so she did. What was the result? Quite soon she came again and said, 'It is extraordinary, when I pray to God, in other words when I talk to him, I feel nothing, but when I sit quietly, face to face with him, then I feel wrapped in his presence.' You will never be able to pray to God really and from all your heart unless you learn to keep silent and rejoice in the miracle of his presence.[7]

This is the heart of the matter. According to classical Christian theology, this is the ultimate end for which we were created. This is the meaning of life.

But what does it mean to enjoy God? This is the dimension of praise, thanksgiving, adoration, worship, contemplation. Too often we think of these as duties. They are not duties but liberties! Christ died not to entangle us in a new set of duties but to set us free to be what we were created for.

a. Thanksgiving

For most of us, praise begins with thanksgiving; with the expression of our gratitude. What could be more natural than thanking God for his good gifts to us?

And yet it does not come naturally. We are tempted to regard expressions of gratitude as servile admissions of inferiority. We are enslaved by our desire for autonomy, for independence.

But, thanks be to God, Christ's death and resurrection sets us free to recognize our dependence on God. As we take time to attend to our dependence on God we will be amazed by his good gifts, by his grace, and the result will be thanksgiving.

b. Adoration

But thanksgiving is only the beginning of praise. Adoration shifts the focus from what God has done for us to God himself. It is the expression of our love for the God who has revealed himself in liberating Israel from Egypt, in the birth, life, death and resurrection of Jesus of Nazareth and in the descent of the Spirit upon the Church at Pentecost.

The Bible offers us a rich vocabulary for expressing our love of God. We can begin to explore the language of adoration with the Psalms and the Song of Solomon. There are also rich resources in the poems and hymns of the Judaeo-Christian traditions on which we may draw. Any hymnbook will provide you with plenty of material. To this you might add the poems of John Donne, George Herbert, Emily Brontë, Gerard Manley Hopkins, T. S. Eliot, R. S. Thomas and countless others. Gradually, as you immerse yourself in their ways of expressing their love for God, you will discover your own vocabulary.

But our praise need not be limited to words. Every aspect of human creativity may be turned into an act of worship. We can express our love for God in music, or painting, or pottery, or sculpture, or dance. And, just as the Spirit may lead us beyond words in intercession, so we may find ourselves praising God in tongues.

Finally there is silence: not an empty silence but the silence of lovers communing together; the silence of a face-to-face encounter with God in Christ. 'For God, who said, "Let light shine out of darkness," [makes] his light shine in our hearts to give us the light of the glory of God in the face of Christ' (2 Cor. 4:6).

c. Praise perfects perfection

Praise is part of a personal relationship. It is not subject to the everyday laws of cause and effect.

Praise is our proper response to God's grace. In praise we are offering back to God what is God's already. But it does not end there. On the contrary, it has only just begun!

God responds to praise with blessing, giving us the resources to find new ways of praising him. And so it goes on. We are caught up into the life of God in an infinite spiral of praise and blessing: we are 'lost in wonder, love and praise.'

Perhaps lack of time and the absence of praise go hand in hand. Busyness certainly suppresses praise. Conversely, we may find that, as we rediscover praise, we will also find enough time for what really matters.

Praise enables us to penetrate to the heart of time. Our created time, our seconds, minutes and hours, are caught up into God's time (or, if you prefer, eternity). Praise is a foretaste of heaven and, ultimately, the only true motive for all Christian activity, all human activity.

8. Exercises

a. *The potter and the clay*

> 'Shall what is formed say to him who formed it, "Why did you make me like this?"' Does not the potter have the right to make out of the same lump of clay some pottery for noble purposes and some for common use? (Rom. 9:20f)

Imagine that you are a lump of clay in the hands of God the potter. Offer yourself up to God's moulding activity. What signs of God's handiwork can you already see in your life?

What would it be like to be so in tune with God's Spirit that everything you did was done with God in mind? Try to imagine such a state. Allow yourself to long for it, with its freedom from busyness; its tranquillity. Turn that longing into a prayer.

b. *Holy expectancy*

Richard Foster suggests that holy expectancy can transform the atmosphere of worship:

> Enter the service ten minutes early. Lift your heart in adoration to the King of Glory. Contemplate His majesty, glory and tenderness as revealed in Jesus Christ. . . . Invite the real Presence to be manifest. Fill the room with Light.
>
> Next, lift into the Light of Christ the pastor or persons with particular responsibilities. Imagine the Shekinah of God's radiance surrounding him or her. Inwardly release them to speak the truth boldly in the power of the Lord.
>
> By now people are beginning to enter. Glance around until your eyes catch some individual who needs your intercessory work. Perhaps their shoulders are drooped, or they seem a bit sad. Lift them into the glorious, refreshing Light of His Presence. Imagine the burden tumbling from their shoulders.[8]

Why not try this at other times as well? Set aside a specific time today to practise the presence of God in this way.

c. Praise the Lord

Read Psalm 103 several times. Saturate yourself in the praises of the psalmist. Let them become your praises. Use them as a launch pad for your own worship – in music, or verse, or dance, or art, or tongues, or whatever medium feels right to you.

> Now to him who is able to do immeasurably more than all we ask or imagine, according to his power that is at work within us, to him be glory in the church and in Christ Jesus throughout all generations, for ever and ever! Amen. (Eph. 3:20f)

Notes

Chapter 1 Time Under Pressure

1. Lewis Carroll, *Alice's Adventures in Wonderland* (Chancellor Press, 1985), pp. 86f.
2. R. Banks, *The Tyranny of Time* (Paternoster, 1983), p. 11.
3. From 'Abide With Me', by H. F. Lyte, *Hymns Ancient and Modern New Standard* (Hymns Ancient and Modern Ltd), no. 27, and other editions.
4. D. Nicholl, *Holiness* (DLT, 1981), p. 74.
5. J. Swift, *Gulliver's Travels* (Peal Press), pp. 25f.
6. E. F. Schumacher, *Good Work* (Harper and Row, 1979), p. 25.
7. R. Feynman, *What Do You Care What Other People Think? Further Adventures of a Curious Character* (Unwin Hyman, 1988), p. 198.
8. P. Thomas, 'The case against an all-day ministry', *Church Times*, 5 June 1992, p. 10.

Chapter 2 Biblical and Theological Perspectives on Time

1. Banks, op. cit., p. 175.
2. C. S. Lewis, *The Screwtape Letters* (Fontana, 1955), p. 107.
3. C. S. Lewis, *Surprised by Joy* (Collins/Fount, 1977).
4. Banks, op. cit., p. 171.
5. P. King, *How Do You Find the Time?* (Pickering and Inglis, 1982), p. 116.
6. O. Guinness, *The Gravedigger File* (Hodder, 1983), p. 64.

NOTES

Chapter 3 How Do We Use Our Time?

1. F. Dewar, *Live for a Change* (DLT, 1988), p. 71.
2. G. Hughes, *God of Surprises* (DLT, 1985), pp. 36f.
3. T. Engstrom, *A Time for Commitment* (MARC, 1988), p. 97.
4. Cited by Banks, op. cit., p. 235.
5. F. Catherwood, *God's Time, God's Money* (Hodders, 1987), p. 29.

Chapter 4 Time for Yourself

1. K. Leech, *Spirituality and Pastoral Care* (Sheldon Press, 1986), pp. 110f.
2. *God's Diverse People* (DLT/Daybreak, 1991).
3. R. Foster, *Celebration of Discipline* (Hodder, 1980), p. 85.
4. See, e.g., Lawrence's *Paper Pilgrimage* (DLT/Daybreak, 1990).
5. G. S. Hendry, *Theology of Nature* (Westminster Press, 1980), p. 13.
6. *As You Like It*, II. vii. 139–43.
7. J. Pieper, *Leisure the Basis of Culture* (Faber and Faber, 1952), pp. 51f.
8. P. King, op. cit., pp. 40f.
9. L. Ryken, *Work and Leisure in Christian Perspective* (IVP, 1989), p. 219.
10. G. MacDonald, *Ordering Your Private World* (Highland Books, 1987), p. 99.
11. Banks, op. cit., p. 61.

Chapter 5 Time for Family and Friends

1. G. MacDonald, *The Effective Father* (Highland Books, 1989), pp. 53f.
2. Cited by Banks, op. cit., p. 50.
3. M. Scott Peck, *The Different Drum* (Rider, 1988), p. 28.
4. R. Van de Weyer, *The Way of Holiness* (Fount, 1992), p. 33.
5. See, e.g., M. Vasey et al, *Family Festivals: An Approach to Worship in the Home* (Grove Books, Worship Series no. 73).
6. Banks, op. cit., p. 239.
7. C. S. Lewis, *The Four Loves* (Fontana, 1963), p. 75.
8. M. Beach, *Sojourners*, Nov. 1979, p. 18.
9. MacDonald, op. cit., p. 118.
10. E. Schaeffer, *What is a Family?* (Hodder, 1978), pp. 153f.

NOTES

Chapter 6 Time for the World

1. H. Nouwen, *Reaching Out* (Fount, 1976), p. 63.
2. L. Newbigin, *Foolishness to the Greeks: The Gospel and Western Culture* (SPCK, 1986), p. 31.
3. S. Turner, *Up To Date: Poems 1968–1982* (Hodder, 1983), p. 45.
4. M. Goodall and J. Reader, 'Creating Spaces' in *The Earth Beneath*, eds. Ball et al (SPCK, 1992), 133–58 (p. 141).
5. D. Nicholl, *The Testing of Hearts: A Pilgrim's Journal* (Lamp Press, 1989), pp. 20f.
6. Nouwen, op. cit., p. 69.
7. Ibid., p. 92.
8. J. Finney, *Finding Faith Today: How does it happen?* (Bible Society, 1992), pp. 43–7.
9. P. Selby, *Liberating God: Private Care and Public Struggle* (SPCK, 1983), p. 36.
10. Goodall and Reader, op. cit., p. 152.
11. E. Schaeffer, *Hidden Art* (Norfolk Press, 1971), pp. 167f.
12. E. Schaeffer, *What is a Family?* p. 169.

Chapter 7 Time for Work

1. P. Sprinkle, *Women Who Do Too Much: Stress and the Myth of the Superwoman* (Zondervan, 1992), p. 102.
2. Cited by J. Seabrook, *The Myth of the Market* (Green Books, 1990), p. 152.
3. MacDonald, *Ordering Your Private World*, p. 184.
4. Cited by B. Walsh, *Subversive Christianity* (Regius Press, 1992), p. 13.
5. D. L. Sayers, *Creed or Chaos* (Harcourt, Brace, 1949), p. 56.
6. Banks, op. cit., p. 214.
7. MacDonald, op. cit., p. 80.
8. E.g., P. Brierley, *Priorities, Planning and Paperwork* (MARC, 1992).
9. Catherwood, op. cit., p. 58.
10. Cited by Banks, op. cit., pp. 22f.

NOTES

Chapter 8 Time for the Church

1. Adapted from P. Hiebert, *Anthropological Insights for Missionaries* (Baker Book House, 1985), pp. 295–7.
2. Guinness, op. cit., p. 90.
3. Cited by Banks, op. cit., p. 209.
4. D. Cormack, *Seconds Away!* (MARC, 1989), pp. 86f.
5. P. and S. Kaldor, *Where the River Flows: Sharing the Gospel in Contemporary Australia* (Lancer, 1988), p. xxiii.

Chapter 9 Time for God

1. From 'The Larger Catechism of the Westminster Divines, 1648', *The Confession of Faith* (William Blackwood and Sons Ltd, 1969), p. 51.
2. *Hymns Ancient and Modern New Standard* (Hymns Ancient and Modern Ltd), no. 240, and other editions.
3. MacDonald, op. cit., p. 24.
4. Cited by S. Magnusson, *The Flying Scotsman* (Quartet Books, 1981), p. 165.
5. B. Hybels, *Too Busy Not to Pray* (IVP, 1989), p. 105.
6. MacDonald, op. cit., pp. 161f.
7. A. Bloom, *Living Prayer* (DLT, 1980), p. 119.
8. Foster, op. cit., p. 142.